ALT+SHIFT+KEY	**CTRL+KEY**	**CTRL+SHIFT+KEY**
Esc	Previous Application	Task	
F1		Speller	Preferences
F2			
F3	Ruler	Refresh Screen	Draft Mode
F4		Close Document	Clear Document
F5	Define Para. Numbering	Date Text	Date Code
F6	Previous Window	Next Document	Previous Document
F7	Decimal Tab	Hanging Indent	Double Indent
F8	Special Codes	Margins	
F9	Columns	Tables	Document Layout
F10		Macro Record	Macro Stop
F11	Text Box Edit	Horizontal Line	Vertical Line
F12	Generate	Merge	Sort

The Sybex Instant Reference Series

Instant References are available on these topics:

Computer users are not all alike.
Neither are SYBEX books.

We know our customers have a variety of needs. They've told us so. And because we've listened, we've developed several distinct types of books to meet the needs of each of our customers. What are you looking for in computer help?

If you're looking for the basics, try the **ABC's** series, or for a more visual approach, select **Teach Yourself.**

Mastering and **Understanding** titles offer you a step-by-step introduction, plus an in-depth examination of intermediate-level features, to use as you progress.

Our **Up & Running** series is designed for computer-literate consumers who want a no-nonsense overview of new programs. Just 20 basic lessons, and you're on your way.

SYBEX **Encyclopedias** and **Desktop References** provide a *comprehensive reference* and explanation of all of the commands, features, and functions of the subject software.

Sometimes a subject requires a special treatment that our standard series doesn't provide. So you'll find we have titles like **Advanced Techniques, Handbooks, Tips & Tricks,** and others that are specifically tailored to satisfy a unique need.

You'll find SYBEX publishes a variety of books on every popular software package. Looking for computer help? Help Yourself to SYBEX.

For a complete catalog of our publications:

SYBEX, Inc.
2021 Challenger Drive, Alameda, CA 94501
Tel: (510) 523-8233/(800) 227-2346 Telex: 336311
Fax: (510) 523-2373

SYBEX is committed to using natural resources wisely to preserve and improve our environment. This is why we have been printing the text of books like this one on recycled paper since 1982.

This year our use of recycled paper will result in the saving of more than 15,300 trees. We will lower air pollution effluents by 54,000 pounds, save 6,300,000 gallons of water, and reduce landfill by 2,700 cubic yards.

In choosing a SYBEX book you are not only making a choice for the best in skills and information, you are also choosing to enhance the quality of life for all of us.

WordPerfect® 5.1 for Windows™ Instant Reference

Alan Simpson

SYBEX®

San Francisco • Paris • Düsseldorf • Soest

Acquisitions Editor: Dianne King
Series Editor: James A. Compton
Editor: Jeff Kapellas
Assistant Editor: Brendan Fletcher
Technical Editor: Sheila Dienes
Word Processors: Ann Dunn and Susan Trybull
Series Design: Ingrid Owen
Screen Graphics: Thomas Goudie
Typesetters: Scott Campbell and Deborah Maizels
Production Editor: Carolina Montilla
Proofreader: David Avilla Silva
Indexer: Julie Kawabata
Cover Designer: Archer Design

Library of Congress Card Number: 91-66939
ISBN: 0-89588-821-1

Manufactured in the United States of America
10 9 8 7 6 5 4 3 2 1

To Susan, Ashley, and Egg #2

Acknowledgments

Every book is a team effort, and this book is certainly no exception. The skills, talents, and hard work of many people brought this book from the idea stage into your hands.

On the publishing side the following people were instrumental in creating this book: Jim Compton, series editor; Jeff Kapellas, editor; Brendan Fletcher, Assistant Editor; Sheila Dienes, technical editor; Ingrid Owen, designer and layout artist; Ann Dunn and Susan Trybull word processors; Scott Campbell and Deborah Maizels, typesetters; Carolina Montilla, production editor; David Avilla Silva, proofreader; Thomas Goudie, screen reproductions and art; and Julie Kawabata, indexer.

On the authorial side, the talented writers Elizabeth Olson, Virginia Anderson, Jan Scholz, and James Patterson provided most of the material in this book; and Martha Mellor miraculously managed all that material.

Bill Gladstone and Matt Wagner of Waterside Productions handled business matters.

Susan and Ashley provided love, support, sustenance, comfort, and lots of patience.

Table of Contents

INTRODUCTION

WordPerfect Corporation has taken all of the best features of the graphical user interface of the 1990s, and incorporated them beautifully into their now-legendary WordPerfect word processing program. Both beginners and old hands alike will appreciate the intuitive, interactive means of creating and editing documents that WordPerfect for Windows brings to the personal computer.

WHOM THIS BOOK IS FOR

This book is designed for WordPerfect users who are "on the go." Its portable, yet comprehensive, format provides ready access to all those big features and little details that are so easily forgotten. Of course, the compact size of this book does not allow for lengthy tutorials about every WordPerfect feature. So if you're new to WordPerfect or Windows, you may want to back this book up with a more comprehensive tutorial, such as *Mastering WordPerfect 5.1 for Windows*, also published by SYBEX.

HOW TO USE THIS BOOK

This book is organized as an encyclopedic reference, with topics arranged alphabetically. Each reference section includes (as appropriate):

- A general description of the feature
- Step-by-step instructions for the use of the feature
- Notes providing additional usage tips and suggestions
- Cross-references to related topics and features

To speed things along, we often present a series of menu selections with an arrow (➤) separating each option, with the optional letter choice for each option in boldface. If the command has a shortcut key sequence, we'll present it in parentheses, like this:

Choose Layout ➤ **M**argins (Ctrl+F8).

You can use any of the usual Windows techniques for choosing these menu options: the mouse, the arrow keys, and the keyboard. If you are not already familiar with these techniques, perhaps your best starting point would be to refer to the sections titled "Mouse" and "Menus" in this book.

SYSTEM REQUIREMENTS

To use WordPerfect for Windows, your computer must first have the following hardware and software configuration:

- An 80286, 80386, or 80486 processor

- At least 2MB Random Access Memory

- A graphics adapter supporting EGA, VGA, 8514/A (1024 x 768), or Hercules graphics

- A hard disk with at least 6MB available storage

- Windows version 3.0 or higher

Though not essential, a mouse is highly recommended, since some features are not accessible without it.

INSTALLING WORDPERFECT FOR WINDOWS

Like any software product, WordPerfect for Windows needs to be installed on your computer before you can use it (you need only install the program once). To install WordPerfect for Windows:

1. Start your computer normally, and go to the DOS command prompt (typically C>).

2. Insert the WordPerfect for Windows Install/Program—1 disk into drive A or B.

3. Type **A:INSTALL** (or **B:INSTALL**, if the disk is in drive B) and press ↵.

4. Follow the instructions that appear on your screen. (You can choose **B**asic when given the option to install the entire program on drive C.)

STARTING WORDPERFECT FOR WINDOWS

To start WordPerfect for Windows, you can either type **WIN WPWIN** and press ↵ at the DOS command prompt, or:

1. Start Windows in the usual manner (by typing **win**).
2. Double-click the WordPerfect group icon in the Program Manager window.
3. Double-click the WordPerfect program item icon in the group window.

The first time you run WordPerfect for Windows, you'll be prompted for your license number, which is printed on the Certificate of License registration card that came with your WordPerfect for Windows package. Type the license number and click OK or press ↵.

WORDPERFECT VS. CUA KEYBOARDS

WordPerfect for Windows follows the Common User Access (CUA) guidelines shared by all Windows applications. However, the program also offers an optional "soft keyboard" that follows, insofar as possible, the cursor-positioning and shortcut keystrokes of earlier versions of WordPerfect.

In this book, we assume that you will be using the default Common User Access (CUA) keyboard. *If you have any problems duplicating the instructions presented in this book, it may be that the optional Word-Perfect for DOS keyboard is in use.* To switch back to the default CUA keyboard:

1. Choose **File** ➤ **Preferences** ➤ **Keyboard**.
2. Click the **Default** (CUA) button (or press Alt+D).
3. Click OK or press ↵.

The CUA keystrokes will then work properly, and the pull-down menus will show the appropriate shortcut keys.

SUMMARY OF NEW AND MODIFIED FEATURES

For experienced WordPerfect users, the section below summarizes some of new and modified features in WordPerfect for

Windows. You can find additional information about each topic under the appropriate heading in this book.

New or Modified Feature	Description
Auto Code Placement	Automatically places certain formatting codes at the beginning of the paragraph or page and replaces the existing code
Button Bar	Lets you convert commonly used menu options and macros to buttons that are readily available on the screen
Convert	Supports more foreign file formats and can be accessed while opening or saving a file, without using an external conversion program
Cut and Paste	Passes text to be moved or copied to the Windows Clipboard, making it easier to cut and paste between documents, as well as between Windows applications
Dynamic Data Exchange (DDE Link)	Links data and graphics from other Windows applications into a WordPerfect document
File Manager	Replaces List Files and can be used outside of WordPerfect any time that Windows is running
Font Selection	Enables you to change the font of selected text without changing the base font for all text beyond the insertion point

Fonts	Allows you to use WordPerfect or Windows fonts; to reuse your WordPerfect 5.1 fonts without re-installing them, copy the existing .PRS and .ALL files from your WordPerfect 5.1 directory to the WordPerfect Corporation Shared Programs (\WPC) directory
Graphical User Interface	Displays graphics, graphic lines, fonts, and other features clearly on your screen; you can, however, use *Draft Mode* when you want to work only with the text
Graphics	Allows you to interactively size and position graphics with your mouse
Macros	Allows you to attach macros to menus, the Button Bar, or certain keys; does not support Alt+*key* macros
Multiple Documents	Allows you to edit up to nine documents at once, with each document in a separate *document window* that can be moved, sized, opened, and closed with the usual Windows techniques
Preferences	Replaces Setup as the means of changing defaults; you can also use screen colors defined in the Windows Control Panel
Print Preview	Replaces View Document, and is still required to see some formatting features, such as headers, footers, and footnotes
Printer Control	Background printing is handled by the Windows Print Manager

Printer Drivers	Allows you to use either WordPerfect or Windows printer drivers
Quick List	Lets you replace any DOS path name, like C:\WPWIN\ LETTERS, with a plain English name, like "Letters and Memos"
Retrieve	**File ➤ Retrieve** now *combines* documents; **File ➤ Open** opens an existing document in a new document window; **File ➤ New** starts a new document
Ruler	Provides a more interactive and intuitive means of changing tab stops, margins, and columns; as well as shortcuts for choosing frequently used features
Special Characters	Special characters can be selected from a menu, without knowing the character's code
Select Text	The term *select* replaces *block*; you can use your mouse, the F8 key, or the Shift+*arrow* keys to select text
Undo	Enables you to undo your most recent change to a document, including formatting changes

ADVANCE

The Advance command lets you place text at a specific place on the current page.

To Position Text on the Page

1. Position the insertion point to the page on which you want to position text.

2. Choose Layout ➤ Advance.

3. Choose the direction in which to move the text.

Up	Moves text up in relation to the current position.
Down	Moves text down in relation to the current position.
To Line	Moves text to a specific line position in relation to the top edge of the page.
Left	Moves text left in relation to the current position.
Right	Moves text right in relation to the current position.
To Position	Moves text to a specific character (horizontal) position in relation to the left edge of the page.

4. Enter the distance by which to move the text in inches (such as **3.5** for 3½ inches), or in points followed by *p* (such as **12p** for 12 points), or enter the line measurement or character position in inches.

5. Repeat steps 3–4 as needed, then press ↵ or click OK.

● **NOTES**   If you want to resume printing at the original print position after using Advance, you must repeat the steps above to insert codes that reposition the printer to where you want to resume printing.

To position text inside a graphic, the Wrap Text Around Box option for the graphic must be unchecked or turned off.

● **EXAMPLE**   The banner in Figure 1 is in a graphic Figure Box with the Wrap Text Around Box option unchecked. The word *Welcome* is in a borderless User Box, and Advance codes within that User Box position the text to fit precisely within the banner. Both boxes are in the same position, and are the same size. If you want text to wrap around the entire image, leave the Wrap Text Around Box option for the User box checked (only text outside the box will wrap; text within the box is not affected.)

See Also   Graphics and Graphic Boxes

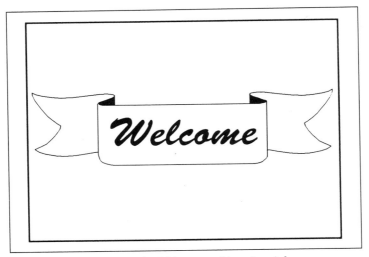

Figure 1: Text positioned within a graphic using Advance

APPEND

The Append command adds selected text or graphics to the clipboard. You can also use the command to bypass the clipboard and append text or graphics directly to the end of a file.

To Add Elements to the Clipboard

1. Select the desired text or graphics.

2. Choose Edit ➤ Append.

The appended material remains on the clipboard until you replace it with Cut or Copy or exit Windows.

To Append Elements to File

1. Select the desired text or graphics.

2. Choose File ➤ Save (Shift+F3).

3. In the Save Selected Text dialog box, type or select the name of the destination file. If the file is not in your default directory, type the full path or use the **D**irectories list box or **Q**uick List check box to locate the file.

4. Choose **S**ave.

5. If the file exists, choose **A**ppend from the Overwrite/Append File dialog box; otherwise, WordPerfect will create a new file and the dialog box will not appear.

● **NOTES**   All attributes of the appended text or graphics, such as boldface or italics, are preserved when appended to the clipboard.

If you want the selected text or graphics to appear in a location other than at the end of your file, append it to the clipboard, then paste it in the desired position.

See Also   Combine Documents

AUTO CODE PLACEMENT

When enabled, the Auto Code Placement command automatically places a formatting code at the beginning of a paragraph or page, regardless of the position of the insertion point. Formatting codes control such factors as column size, letter spacing, line numbering, margin settings, and tab settings.

To Enable the Auto Code Placement

1.   Choose File ➤ Preferences ➤ Environment.

2.   Select or deselect the Auto Code Placement switch in the dialog box.

3.   Choose OK.

With Auto Code Placement enabled, most formatting codes are placed at the beginning of the paragraph and affect the entire paragraph. The codes for the top and bottom margins, page numbering, and page format suppression are placed at the beginning of the page and affect the entire page. The code stays in effect until the end of the document unless the code occurs again.

With the Auto Code Placement turned off, the code takes effect at the insertion point and remains in effect until the end of the document, unless another code of the same kind is encountered.

● **NOTES**   If a paragraph or page of text has been selected prior to code insertion, the entire paragraph or page will be affected.

AUTOMATIC BACKUP

WordPerfect can automatically back up files in two ways: by saving documents at timed intervals, and by saving a copy of the original file each time you replace the original with a newer version.

To Control Timed and Original Backups

1. Select File ➤ Preferences ➤ Backup.

2. Select one of the following options: (you may use both at the same time):

Timed Document Backup	Make timed backups.
Original Document Backup	Back up the original file.

3. For Timed Document Backup, enter the number of minutes between backups. The default is 20 minutes.

4. Choose OK or ↵.

● **NOTES**   Timed backups are saved in temporary files named WP{WP}.BK1 and WP{WP}.BK2 for Doc 1 and Doc 2, respectively. These backups are deleted when you exit WordPerfect normally, but stay on disk if a power failure or other problem terminates Word-Perfect abnormally.

Timed backup files are stored in the same directory as your WP.EXE program. If you want to store them in a separate directory, select File ➤ Preferences ➤ Location of Files ➤ Backup Files. Enter the name of the directory where you want to save timed backup files.

If the timed backup files exist the next time you start WordPerfect, you'll be asked to rename, open, or delete them before being taken to the document window. If you retrieve them, you may then recover all your work up to the moment of interruption. If you elect to delete them, they are lost forever.

Original backups are always stored in the same directory as your document file. The old version of the original file is named <filename>.BK! and will remain on disk after you exit WordPerfect. Note that all original backup files have the same extension so if you have files with the same file name but different extensions, only one will have an original backup file—the last one that was edited.

When you recover an original backup file, rename it immediately to remove the .BK! extension.

See Also   File Manager, Preferences, Save/Save As

BINDING OFFSET

The Binding Offset command shifts text on the page to provide extra space for binding on the left edge of odd-numbered pages and on the right edge of even-numbered pages.

To Set a Binding Edge

1.   Select File ➤ Print (F5).

2.   Enter the offset amount in the **B**inding Offset text box.

3.   Choose Close. Or, if you are ready to print the document, choose **Print** or press ↵.

4.   To remove the binding offset, enter an offset of zero (0).

● **NOTES**   Binding offset works together with the Binding feature (Layout ➤ Page ➤ Paper Size). When you set the binding edge at the Left, the binding offset shifts text to the right on odd-numbered pages and to the left on even-numbered pages. When you set the binding edge at the Top, the binding offset shifts text down on odd-numbered pages and up on even-numbered pages.

The binding offset is added to the inside margin and subtracted from the outside. For even margins, enter an offset value that's half of what you actually intend, and add the same amount to both margins (see Example).

The Binding Offset applies to the current document only and is saved with the document. To change it, you must reopen the file, change the offset, and store it again.

● **EXAMPLE**   You want a ½-inch binding offset, binding at the left edge, and 1-inch left and right margins. To achieve this, set the binding offset to 0.25 inch and increase both margins to 1.25 inch.

See Also   Margins, Paper Size, Print, Units of Measure

BORDER STYLES

The Border Styles command sets the appearance of border lines used around graphic boxes and tables from the insertion point position forward.

1. Move the insertion point to where the new settings should take effect.

2. Select **G**raphics.

3. Select the box type to which the border settings will apply, and then select **O**ptions.

4. Select desired border styles from the Left, Right, Top, and Bottom pop-up lists. Selectable attributes are **N**one, **S**ingle, **D**ouble, **D**ashed, **D**otted, **T**hick, and **E**xtra Thick.

5. Specify the distance of the border from the box contents in the Border Spacing area.

6. Press ↵ or choose OK.

● **NOTES** WordPerfect inserts an option code at the insertion point position, and all boxes and tables forward of that position use the new settings. To change the border styles for all future documents, place the option code in the Initial Codes using File ➤ Preferences ➤ Initial Codes.

See Also Graphics and Graphic Boxes, Initial Codes, Tables

BUTTON BAR

The Button Bar contains regularly used menu selections and macros. Three Button Bars are provided by WordPerfect but you can create your own custom Button Bars.

To Display a Button Bar

1.   Choose **View** ➤ Button Bar Setup ➤ Select.

2.   Select the name of the desired Button Bar from the Select Button Bar dialog box (see Options below).

3.   Click on Select to display the Button Bar.

To Create a Custom Button Bar

1.   Choose **View** ➤ Button Bar Setup ➤ New.

2.   Add buttons by choosing any menu item. The button will appear in the bar. You can add as many buttons as you need; the bar will scroll to display the buttons that do not fit on the screen. Click on the arrows at the left of the bar to scroll the bar.

3.   To remove a button, drag the button off the bar.

4.   To rearrange the buttons, drag the button to the new position. The other buttons will move to make room for the inserted button.

5.   When you have finished adding buttons to the bar, click on OK to save the bar.

6.   You will be asked to name the bar. Enter a name in the Save As text box. Then click **Save** or press ↵.

To Edit an Existing Button Bar

1.   Choose **View** ➤ Button Bar Setup ➤ Edit.

2.   Add, rearrange, or delete buttons as described in the section above and click OK.

To Assign a Macro to a Button

1.   Choose **View** ➤ Button Bar Setup ➤ Edit.

2.   Click on **A**ssign Macro to Button in the dialog box.

3. Select the name of the macro to assign to the button.

4. Click on **A**ssign and then OK.

● **OPTIONS**   The Button Bar may be displayed at the top, bottom, left, or right of the screen. It may also be displayed with text only, icons only, or with both text and pictures. These options are set by choosing View ➤ Button Bar Setup ➤ Options and selecting the appropriate option from the dialog box.

Figure 2 illustrates the built-in WordPerfect for Windows button bars:

SECOND.WWB: Offers features related to graphics and the macro recorder.

TABLES.WWB: Offers features for working with tables; these options are available only when the insertion point is within a table.

WP{WP}.WWB: The default WordPerfect for Windows button bar.

CANCEL

Cancel is WordPerfect's universal "get me out of trouble" feature. This option backs out of menu choices, cancels any operation that displays a prompt or menu, and stops a macro or merge operation before it finishes.

To Cancel the Current Operation

You may cancel an operation in one of the following ways:

- Choose Cancel from a dialog box.
- Double-click the Control-menu box.
- With the keyboard, press Escape (Esc).

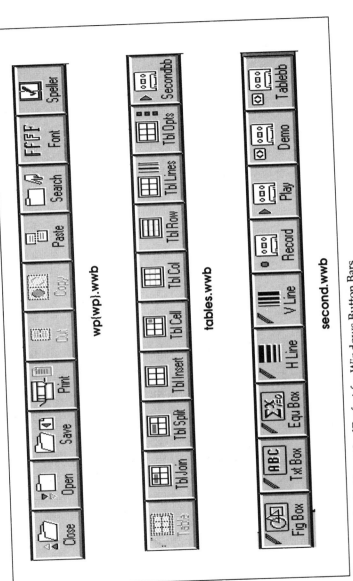

Figure 2: The Built-in WordPerfect for Windows Button Bars

● **NOTES** You may need to cancel more than once when backing out of menus, until you reach the document window.

See Also Document Window, Exit, Undelete

CARTRIDGES AND FONTS

For some printers you can buy additional fonts supplied either on disk (soft or downloadable fonts) or on cartridges (cartridge fonts) that plug into a slot on the printer. To use these fonts with Word-Perfect, you must install them; that is, you must let the program know where to find them.

Use the features described here only if you have purchased soft fonts, cartridges, or additional print wheels for your printer and need to make them available to WordPerfect. To use these features, you must first select the Windows printers driver in the Select File dialog box.

To Install Cartridges and Fonts

1. Choose File ➤ Select Printer.

2. Select the desired printer from the list and choose Setup.

If you are installing cartridges:

3. Scroll through the list of available cartridges. You may select up to two cartridges.

4. Choose Fonts to install cartridge fonts or OK (or press ↵) to return to the Select Printer dialog box.

If you are installing soft fonts:

3. Choose Add Fonts from the Printer Font Installer dialog box.

4. Put the font disk in drive A: (or change the default drive).

5. Choose OK.

6. Select the names of the desired fonts from the displayed list.

7. When all fonts are selected, choose **A**dd.

8. Choose OK to copy the fonts into a WordPerfect directory. By default, this will be C:\PCLFONTS, but you can specify a different path.

9. Choose Close Drive when finished.

If you have installed cartridge fonts, you must select the desired cartridge from the list displayed in the Printer Setup dialog box.

If you have installed soft fonts, you must indicate whether they are to be permanently memory resident or downloaded only when needed. Fonts take up quite a lot a memory so you will want to keep permanent only those fonts you frequently use. When first installed, all soft fonts are considered temporary. To download a soft font permanently:

1. Select the desired font from the list in the Printer Font Installer dialog box. Select only one font at a time.

2. Choose Permanent.

3. Repeat steps 1 and 2 until all permanent fonts have been selected.

4. Choose Exit. The Download Options dialog box will appear.

5. By default, both Download Now and Download at Startup are selected. You can leave them as is or change one of them.

6. Choose OK to return to the Printer Setup dialog box.

To Set the Initial Font

1. Choose File ➤ Select Printer.

2. Choose Initial **F**ont from the dialog box.

3. Select the desired font and point size from the displayed lists in the Printer Initial Font dialog box.

4. Choose OK or press ↵.

To Delete a Soft Font

1. Choose File ➤ Select Printer.
2. Choose Setup, then Fonts.
3. Select the soft fonts to delete from the list.
4. Choose Delete.
5. Choose Yes to delete fonts from both the hard disk and the printer. Or choose No to delete them from only the printer. Although the font name will not appear on the list, it will remain on the hard disk.
6. Choose OK to return to the Select Printer dialog box.

See Also   Font, Location of Files, Paper Size, Printer Select

CASE CONVERSION

This command converts selected text to uppercase or lowercase letters.

To Convert the Case of Selected Text

1. Select the text whose case you want to convert.
2. Choose Edit ➤ Convert Case.
3. Choose either Uppercase or Lowercase.

● **NOTES**   Converting text to lowercase generally does not affect a capital letter at the beginning of a sentence or following a period. Be sure to include the preceding punctuation so that the first word is recognized as the beginning of a sentence. (A capital letter beginning a paragraph, however, will be converted.) In addition, the word "I" and words that begin with "I" followed by an apostrophe are not converted to lowercase.

See Also   Selecting Text

CENTER

This command centers text horizontally between margins or within columns.

To Center One Line of Text

1. Position the insertion point at the place where you want to center new text or to the left of existing text. The existing text should be at the beginning of a line.

2. Choose Layout ➤ Line ➤ Center (Shift+F7). The text will center between the margins.

3. If you want dot leaders, repeat step 2.

4. If you are centering new text, type the new text and press ↵.

5. To continue the dots to the right of the text, position the insertion point at the end of the text. Choose Layout ➤ Line ➤ Flush Right ➤ Layout ➤ Line ➤ Flush Right (Alt+F7,Alt+F7).

To Center Text On a Specific Location

To center text at a particular line position or in a column, position the insertion point at the desired center point (at least two spaces from the left margin) before choosing Center.

To Center Large Sections of Text

1. Position the insertion point above the text to be centered.

2. Choose Layout ➤ Justification ➤ Center, or press Ctrl+J. The text will center horizontally to the next justification code or the end of the document.

● **NOTES**   To center text vertically (top to bottom) on the page, see Center Page.

See Also   Center Page, Justification, Page Breaks, Selecting
Text, Tabs

CENTER PAGE

This command centers all text on the page between the top and bottom margins.

To Center Text Vertically

1. Position the insertion point at the top of the page of text to be centered, before any other codes.

2. Choose Layout ➤ Page (Alt+F9).

3. Choose Center Page.

● **NOTES**   If additional text follows the text to be centered vertically (for example, a document that follows a centered title page), move the insertion point to the end of the vertically centered text and insert a hard page break (Layout ➤ Page ➤ Page Break, or Ctrl+⏎).

If Auto Code Placement is set on, you can place the insertion point anywhere on the page and the [Center Pg] code will be put at the top of the page.

See Also   Auto Code Placement, Center

CODES

Formatting in a document is controlled by hidden codes, visible only on the Reveal Codes screen. Codes that affect all text beyond them are single codes. Codes that affect individual blocks of text are paired codes as indicated by the words on and off. For example, the

[Ln Spacing 2] code below double-spaces all text below the code (up to the next [Ln Spacing] code, if any), and the [Italc On] and [Italc Off] codes italicize the words *Getting Started*.

(Ln Spacing: 2)(Italc On)Getting Started(Italc Off): To start the engine, insert the key and turn to the right.

● **NOTES** Codes are inserted automatically when you press a formatting key (such as Tab or ↵), or when you choose formatting options from the menus. Table 1 summarizes the WordPerfect for Windows codes.

See Also Reveal Codes

Table 1: WordPerfect for Windows formatting codes

Code	Definition
[–]	Hyphen character
[AdvDn]	Advance down a specified distance
[AdvUp]	Advance up a specified distance
[AdvLft]	Advance left a specified distance
[AdvRgt]	Advance right a specified distance
[AdvToLn]	Advance vertically
[AdvToPos]	Advance horizontally
[BLine On/Off]	Baseline placement
[Block Pro]	Block protection
[Bold On/Off]	Boldface
[Box Num]	Caption in graphics box
[Cell]	Table cell
[Center]	Center
[Center Pg]	Center page vertically
[Cndl EOP]	Conditional end of page
[Cntr Tab]	Centered tab

Table 1: WordPerfect for Windows formatting codes (continued)

Code	Definition
[Col Def]	Column definition
[Col Off]	End of text columns
[Col On]	Beginning of text columns
[Color]	Print color
[Comment]	Document comment
[Date]	Date/Time function
[Dbl Indent]	Double Indent
[Dbl Und On/Off]	Double underline
[DDE Link Begin/End]	DDE Link
[Dec Tab]	Decimal-aligned tab
[Decml/Algn Char]	Decimal character/thousands separator
[Def Mark:Index]	Index definition
[Def Mark:List]	List definition
[Def Mark:ToA]	Table of Authorities definition
[Def Mark:ToC]	Table of Contents definition
[Dorm HRt]	Dormant hard return
[DSRt]	Deletable soft return
[Embedded]	Embedded code
[End C/A]	End of Centering/Alignment
[End Def]	End of definition
[End Mark]	End of mark
[End Opt]	Endnote options
[Endnote]	Endnote
[Endnote Placement]	Endnote placement

Table 1: WordPerfect for Windows formatting codes (continued)

Code	Definition
[Equ Box]	Equation box
[Equ Opt]	Equation box options
[Ext Large On/Off]	Extra-large print
[Fig Box]	Figure box
[Fig Opt]	Figure box options
[Fine On/Off]	Fine print
[Flsh Rgt]	Flush right
[Font]	Base font
[Footer A/B]	Footer A/B
[Footnote]	Footnote
[Force]	Force odd/even page
[Ftn Opt]	Footnote options
[Full Form]	Table of authorities, full form
[HdCntrTab]	Hard center tab
[HdDecTab]	Hard decimal-aligned tab
[HdRgtTab]	Hard right tab
[HdSpc]	Hard space
[HdTab]	Hard (left) tab
[Header A/B]	Header A/B
[HLine]	Horizontal line
[HPg]	Hard page break
[Hrd Row]	Hard row
[HRt]	Hard return
[Hrt-SPg]	Hard return - soft page break
[Hyph On/Off]	Hyphenation
[HyphSRt]	Hyphenation soft return
[HyphIgnWrd]	Hyphenation ignore word

Table 1: WordPerfect for Windows formatting codes (continued)

Code	Definition
[HZone]	Hyphenation zone
[Indent]	Indent
[Index]	Index entry
[Insert Pg Num]	Insert page number
[ISRt]	Invisible soft return
[Italc On/Off]	Italics
[Just]	Justification specification
[Just Lim]	Word-spacing justification limits
[Kern On/Off]	Kerning
[L/R Mar]	Left & right margin settings
[Lang]	Language
[Large On/Off]	Large print
[Line Height Adj]	Line height adjustment
[Link]	Spreadsheet link
[Link End]	End of link
[Ln Height]	Line height
[Ln Num On/Off]	Line numbering
[Ln Spacing]	Line spacing
[Mar Rel]	Left margin release
[Mark:List]	List entry
[Mark:ToA]	Table of Authorities entry
[Mark:ToC]	Table of Contents entry
[Mrg:PAGEOFF]	Merge page off
[New End Num]	New endnote number
[New Equ Num]	New Equation box number
[New Fig Num]	New Figure box number

Table 1: WordPerfect for Windows formatting codes (continued)

Code	Definition
[New Ftn Num]	New footnote number
[New Tbl Num]	New table number
[New Txt Num]	New Text box number
[New Usr Num]	New User box number
[Note Num]	Footnote number
[Open Style]	Open document style
[Outline On/Off]	Outline
[Ovrstk]	Overstrike characters
[Paper Sz/Typ]	Paper size and type
[Par Num]	Paragraph number
[Par Num Def]	Paragraph numbering definition
[Pg Num]	New page number
[Pg Num Style]	Page number style
[Pg Numbering]	Page number position
[Ptr Cmnd]	Printer command
[Redln On/Off]	Redline
[Ref:*Reference type*]	Reference tied to a specific type
[Rgt Tab]	Right tab
[Row]	Table row
[Shadw On/Off]	Shadow
[Sm Cap On/Off]	Small caps
[Small On/Off]	Small print
[SPg]	Soft page break
[SRt]	Soft return

Table 1: WordPerfect for Windows formatting codes (continued)

Code	Definition
[Stkout On/Off]	Strikeout
[Style On/Off]	Style
[Subdoc]	Subdocument
[Subdoc End]	End of subdocument
[Subdoc Start]	Beginning of subdocument
[Subscpt On/Off]	Subscript
[Suppress]	Suppress page format
[Suprscpt On/Off]	Superscript
[Tab]	Tab
[Tab Set]	Tab set
[T/B Mar]	Top and bottom margins
[Target]	Target (cross-reference)
[Tbl Box]	Table box
[Tbl Def]	Table definition
[Tbl Off]	End of table
[Tbl Opt]	Table box options
[ToA]	Table of authorities
[Text Box]	Text box
[Txt Opt]	Text box options
[Und On/Off]	Underlining
[Undrln]	Underline spaces/tabs
[Usr Box]	User-defined box
[Usr Opt]	User-defined box options
[VLine]	Vertical line
[Vry Large On/Off]	Very large print

Table 1: WordPerfect for Windows formatting codes (continued)

Code	Definition
[W/O On/Off]	Widow/orphan
[Wrd/Ltr Spacing]	Word and letter spacing

COLUMNS

The Columns command lets you create multiple columns of text.

To Define Columns

1. Move the insertion point to where the columns should begin.

2. Choose Layout ➤ Columns (Alt+Shift+F9).

3. Choose Define.

4. Choose one or more of the column definition options described below. WordPerfect inserts a [Col Def] code at the insertion point position.

5. If you want to begin columns at this point, choose OK. Otherwise, press Cancel to return to the document window.

Options   Choose one or more of these options when defining columns:

• Number of Columns: Enter a number between 2 and 24.

- Type (specify one of the following):

Newspaper	"Snaking" columns, in which text ends at the bottom of one column and resumes at the top of the next column.
Parallel	Each column is printed independently, side-by-side on a page; each column's text carries over to the next page.
Parallel with **B**lock Protect	This format is the same as parallel, except that the full block of side-by-side columns stays together and the whole block moves to the next page if the one column spills over.

- **M**argins: This option enables you to manually set the left and right margin for each column. This is useful if you want columns with different widths.

- **D**istance Between Columns: Specify the distance between columns (in inches) to automatically set the left and right margin settings for all columns. Or select **E**venly Spaced for automatic spacing.

To Use the Ruler to Define Columns

You can also define columns by clicking the Column button on the ruler Button Bar. Select the number of columns from the pop-up menu and the ruler margin bar will show the columns evenly spaced across the page. If you want to vary the column spacing, drag the margin markers to the desired position.

To Turn Columns On

Make sure the insertion point is at the location where you want the columns to begin, to the right of the [Col Def] code. Then either click the ruler column button and select Columns On, or choose Layout ➤ Columns (Alt+Shift+F9), and then choose Columns **O**n.

WordPerfect inserts a [Col On] code, and all text after the insertion point is placed into columns (up to the next [Col Off] code.)

To Turn Columns Off

Click on the ruler column button and select Columns Off, or choose Layout ➤ Columns (Alt+Shift+F9), and then choose Columns Off.

WordPerfect inserts a [Col Off] code, which resumes normal (non-columnar) format.

To Edit Columns

To edit text in column format, use the standard editing and insertion point positioning techniques, with these exceptions:

- Choose Layout ➤ Page ➤ Page Break (Ctrl+↵) to start a new column. Newspaper columns are started automatically when you reach the bottom of a page, but you may start a new column earlier by inserting a page break. In parallel columns, a page break moves to the next column.

- To move from column to column without inserting text, use your mouse normally, or press Alt+← or Alt+→, depending on which column you want to move to.

To Redefine the Number of Columns

To reduce the number of columns, use the ruler Column buttons pop-up menu. To delete all columns, turn on Reveal Codes and delete the column definition code [Col Def] and its associated Hard Page Break codes [HPg]. To add another column, use the ruler's Column button and select another number of columns from the pop-up menu, or use Layout ➤ Columns ➤ Define to change the number of columns.

● **NOTES**   You can set columnar format after you have entered text and graphics. Just be sure the codes are in this order: Column Definition [Col Def], Column On [Col On], text and graphics, Column Off [Col Off]. Use Reveal Codes to examine the order and position of the codes.

You cannot use columns within footnotes, endnotes, or tables.

● **EXAMPLE** Figure 3 shows newspaper-style columns in a newsletter. Figure 4 shows parallel columns with margin notes in the left columns and body (main) text in the right column.

See Also Insertion Point, Reveal Codes, Tables, Units of Measure

COMBINE DOCUMENTS

You may combine WordPerfect files in two ways: by inserting the new file into the current document or by appending it to the end of the document (see the Append command reference).

To Insert a File into the Current Document

1. Position the insertion point at the location where you want to add the file.

2. Choose File ➤ Retrieve.

3. Select the name of the desired file, changing the directory if necessary, and click **Retrieve**.

4. Choose Yes when asked "Insert file into current document?"

Note that choosing File ➤ Open opens the selected file in a separate window while retrieving a file gives you the option of inserting it into the current document.

See Also Append

CROSS-REFERENCE

You can use automatic cross-referencing features to reference page numbers, paragraph or outline numbers, footnote and endnote numbers, and graphics box numbers.

The Vacationer

Vol. 1 No. 1   Travel fun for everyone   January 1992

Newsletter debut
by Joan Smith

We're pleased to bring this first issue of our newsletter, *The Vacationer*, to our many loyal customers. The newsletter was inspired by your ideas and questions. You've asked us about where to find the best travel fares, where to go for the person who has been everywhere, what to eat and how to eat it when visiting faraway countries. We've responded by creating this newsletter.

Here we'll bring you the latest news about great deals on vacations in exotic corners of our planet, fun places for inexpensive weekend getaways, and out-of-the-way spots you might never have thought to ask us about. We'll include handy vacation planning tips and introduce you to exciting foods, puzzling customs, and important laws you'll encounter during sojourns to foreign lands. So relax, enjoy, and travel with us as we bring you a new issue every season.   ✿

Celebrate with us
by Jill Evans
In honor of our newsletter's maiden voyage, we'd like to invite you to an Open House at 7:00pm on January 11, 1991, at our offices. Please dress casually or come in your most fashionable travel togs.   ✿

Tropical travel
by Elizabeth Olson

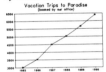

Vacation Trips to Paradise
(booked by our office)

Travel to tropical islands is on the increase. Just look at the graph showing our

---

Inside...

Figure 3: Newspaper-style columns

Using Parallel Columns

This small passage illustrates a practical application of parallel columns; margin notes in the left column. This main body text is in the right column, the margin note is in the left column.

Use parallel columns when you want to create a lengthy document with text that wraps within its own column.

In this example, parallel columns were defined at the top of the document. To insert a heading that cuts across the columns, turn columns off just above the heading. Then turn columns back on beneath the heading to return to your two-column format. You can use styles to define the format of various elements (headings, margin notes, body text). To simplify matters, you can create a macro that initiates each style, including shifting the margin note into the left column.

Figure 4: Parallel columns

You can mark references and targets in the same operation, or you can mark them separately. A target is the place (such as a page number, figure, or table) where you are sending the reader. Each target will have a target name.

Just before printing the document, generate the cross-references so they accurately reflect the numbering of pages, figures, tables, and so on.

To Mark Both the Reference and Target

1.   Move the insertion point to the location where you want to create the reference.

2.   Type any introductory text, such as **(see page**.

3.   Choose Tools ➤ Mark Text ➤ Cross-Reference (F12,R).

4.   Select **R**eference and Target.

5.   Choose a reference type from the Tie Reference to pop-up menu (see Notes below).

6.   Enter a target name and select OK.

7. Click OK in the Mark Cross Reference Both dialog box, then move the insertion point to just after the target and press Enter. See Notes for exceptions.

8. If necessary, finish typing the introductory text for the reference, such as **)**.

To Mark the Reference Only

1. Move the insertion point to the location where you want to create the reference.

2. Type any introductory text.

3. Choose **Tools** ➤ Mark Text ➤ Cross-**R**eference (F12,R).

4. Select **R**eference.

5. Choose a reference type from the Tie Reference To pop-up menu.

6. Enter a target name and select OK.

7. If necessary, finish typing the introductory text.

To Mark the Target Only

1. Move the insertion point to just after the target (see Notes).

2. Choose **Tools** ➤ Mark Text ➤ Cross-**R**eference (F12,R).

3. Select **T**arget.

4. Enter a target name and select OK.

To Generate Cross-References

1. Choose **Tools** ➤ Generate (Alt+F12).

2. Click **Y**es.

● **NOTES**   WordPerfect maintains cross-references automatically, so you may make as many changes as you like and still keep the cross-references accurate. You can create cross-references for an individual document or for a master document (see the Master Document command reference).

To delete a cross reference or target, delete the appropriate [Ref] or [Target] code. Use the Reveal Codes command (Alt+F3) to help you locate the codes in the text.

References   References tell the reader to look somewhere else, as in "see Figure x" or "see Footnote x." You can use the Reference Only procedures if you've already marked the target and need to add more references to it. You *must* use References Only for references located in a graphics box caption, header, or footer.

For graphics boxes, the caption number style (e.g., "Figure 1") is automatically inserted as introductory text; for page numbers, the page number style (e.g., "Page 1") is automatically inserted.

Available reference types are Page Number, Paragraph/Outline, Footnote Number, Endnote Number, Figure, Table Box, Text Box, User Box, or Equation Box.

Targets   Use the Target Only procedures if you've already marked references but haven't yet marked their targets.

Because the target name ties the reference and target together, the name you assign when marking a target must match the name you use when marking references to that target.

You normally place the insertion point just after the target you want to mark. There are three exceptions to this rule:

- To mark page numbers, move the insertion point within the text of the target, not after it.

- To mark a page number for a footnote or endnote, display the footnote or endnote in its editing screen before marking the target (choose Layout ➤ Footnote ➤ Edit, or Layout ➤ Endnote ➤ Edit).

- To mark a page number for a graphics box, place the target in the graphics box caption (choose Graphics ➤ *graphic type* ➤ Caption).

Multiple Cross-References   You can create two types of multiple cross-references:

- References to a target with multiple reference types (e.g., *see page 1, Figure 2*). To do this, mark several cross-references, each with different reference types (e.g., page, graphics box, footnote number). Each reference should give the same target name.

- References to multiple targets with the same reference type (e.g., *see pages 10, 12, 14*). To do this, mark one cross reference, but create multiple targets all with the same target name.

See Also   Footnotes and Endnotes, Generate, Graphics and Graphic Boxes, Master Document, Outline, Page Numbering, Tables

CUT AND PASTE

This procedure allows you to move or copy selected text and graphics within and between documents, including those in other Windows applications. Copying selected text leaves the original text intact while cutting removes it from its original position.

To Cut and Paste Within One Document

1. Select the text or graphics to cut or copy.

2. Choose Edit ➤ Cut (Shift+Del), or Edit ➤ Copy (Ctrl+Ins).

3. Move the insertion point to the place you want the text to appear.

4. Choose Edit ➤ Paste (Shift+Ins).

To Cut and Paste between Documents

1. Select the text or graphics to be cut or copied.

2. Choose Edit ➤ Cut (Shift+Del) or Edit ➤ Paste (Shift+Ins).

3. Open the document file in which you want to insert the text and position the insertion point where the text is to appear.

4. Choose Edit ➤ Paste (Shift+Ins).

To Cut and Paste with Other Windows Applications

1. Select the text or graphics to be cut or copied.

2. Choose Edit ➤ Cut (Shift+Del) or Edit ➤ Copy (Ctrl+Ins).

3. Open the destination Windows application and file into which you want to insert the text.

4. Position the insertion point where the material is to appear.

5. Choose Paste from the application Edit menu.

See Also   Selecting Text

DATE/TIME OPERATIONS

With these procedures, you can insert the current date and time into a document and format it.

You can enter the date either as a code or as text. If you enter a code for date and time, it will automatically be updated to reflect the current system time whenever you retrieve or print the document. However, date and time entered as text will *not* change when you retrieve or print the document. (The system date and time are determined by the DOS commands DATE and TIME. See your DOS manual.)

To Set the Date/Time Format for the Current Document

1. Choose Tools ➤ Date ➤ Format.

2. Select from Predefined Dates, Date Codes, and Time Codes drop-down lists or enter the desired date format coding in the edit line. Table 2 shows the available date and time format codes.

3. Press ⏎ or click OK.

To Set the Default Date/Time Format

1. Choose File ➤ Preferences ➤ Date Format.

2. Set the date and time format as outlined above.

3. Press ⏎ or click OK.

To Insert the Date and Time in a Document

1. If necessary, set the date and/or time format as outlined above.

2. Choose Tools ➤ Date ➤ Text (Ctrl+F5) to enter the date/time as text, or Tools ➤ Date ➤ Code (Ctrl+Shift+F5) to enter it as a code.

● **NOTES** Table 2 lists the codes that define date and time formats; Table 3 presents examples of their use.

Table 2: Codes for defining date and time formats

Code	Meaning
[Day #]	Day of the month
[Month #]	Month number
[Month]	Month name (e.g., July)
[Abbr. Month]	Abbreviated month name (e.g., Sep)
[Year ##]	Year (last 2 digits)
[Year ####]	Year (all 4 digits)
[Weekday]	Day of the week (name, e.g., Monday)
[Abbr. Weekday]	Abbreviated day of the week (e.g., Mon)
[Hour[12]#]	12-hour clock hour number

Table 2: Codes for defining date and time formats (continued)

Code	Meaning
[Hour[24]#]	24-hour clock hour number
[Minute #]	Minute number
[AM/PM]	AM/PM mark
0 or _	Used before a number symbol (#), will pad numbers with fewer than two digits with a leading zero or space, respectively.

Table 3: Examples using date and time character formats

Type this	To get a date or time like this
[Month][Day #],[Year ####]	January 4, 1992
[Abbr. Weekday], [Abbr. Month] [Day #], [Year ####]	Sat, Jan 4, 1992
[Hour[12]#]:[Minute #] [AM/PM]	4:30pm
[Month 0#]/[Day 0#]/[Year ##] ([Hour[12]#]:[Minute #] [AM/PM])	01/04/92 (4:30pm)
[Month #]/[Day_#]/[Year ##] (Hour[12]#]:[Minute #] [AM/PM])	1/ 4/92 (4:30pm)

See Also   Print, Retrieve

DECIMAL ALIGNMENT

You can change the decimal align character (initially ".") used in tabs and tables, and the thousands separator (initially ",") used in math calculations.

To Change the Alignment Character in the Current Document

1.   Move the insertion point to the location where the new characters should take effect.

2.   Choose Layout ➤ Line ➤ Special Codes (Shift+F9,O).

3.   Click the Decimal Align Character button and enter one character.

4.   To change the thousands separator as well, move the insertion point to the Thousands Separator Character text box and enter a new character.

5.   Press ↵ or click Insert.

To leave a setting unchanged in step 3 or 4, just press Escape or choose Cancel.

● **NOTES**   You can change the initial alignment character or thousands separator for all documents. Use File ➤ Preferences ➤ Initial Codes and then select Layout ➤ Line ➤ Special Codes.

See Also   Initial Codes, Tabs

DELETE OPERATIONS

These procedures let you delete text and codes. See the File Manager command reference for information on deleting files, and the Move command reference for details on deleting selected text, sentences, paragraphs, and pages.

To Delete Text or Codes

1. Move the insertion point to the text or codes you want to delete.

2. Use one of the keystrokes listed in Table 4.

To Restore Deleted Text and Codes

1. Move the insertion point to the location where you want to restore the text and codes.

2. Choose Edit ➤ Undelete (Alt+Shift+Backspace).

3. Choose Restore. (See the Undelete command reference for more information.)

● **NOTES**   After you delete text or codes, the remaining text will automatically reformat to match the remaining codes.

To delete a code or item of text globally, use Edit ➤ Replace to find the text you want to delete and, in the Search and Replace dialog box, just leave the Replace With text box empty.

Table 4: Keystrokes for deleting text and codes

To Delete	Press
Character or code to left of the insertion point	Backspace
Character or code at the insertion point	Delete (Del)
Selected text	Delete (Del)
From the insertion point to end of line	Ctrl+Delete (Del)
Word at the insertion point	Ctrl+Backspace

To see the codes you're deleting, turn Reveal Codes on (choose **View** ➤ Reveal **C**odes or press Alt+F3). The code or text at the location of the insertion point appears on a red background. (On a monochrome monitor, the background is reverse-video.) Move the insertion point to the code in the Reveal Codes screen and press the Delete (Del) key.

Deleting one code of a paired code (e.g., [Bold On] or [Bold Off]) automatically deletes both codes of the pair.

See Also   File Manager, Insert, Move, Replace, Reveal Codes, Selecting Text, Undelete

DIALOG BOXES

A dialog box appears whenever you choose a menu option that requires additional information. Figure 5 shows a sample dialog box.

To Move a Dialog Box

If a dialog box is obscuring text that you want to view, you can move it by dragging its title bar to a new location, just as you would a window. Alternatively, open the dialog box's Control menu (if it has one) by clicking its Control-menu box or pressing Alt+spacebar. Choose Move, position the dialog box with the arrow keys, and press ↵.

To Move within a Dialog Box

The current option within a dialog box is highlighted or outlined with a dashed line. You can move from one option to the next by one of three methods:

- Click on the option you want.

- Press Tab (to move forward) or Shift+Tab (to move backward) to the item you want. This method simply highlights the item; you must then click it to select it.

- If the option you want has an underlined letter, you can choose the option by holding down the Alt key and typing the underlined letter in the option name. This method selects the option as well as highlighting it.

To Escape a Dialog Box

Use one of the following methods to escape a dialog box without making choices, or to nullify any current choices:

- Double-click the Control-menu box.

- Press the Escape (Esc) key.

- Click the Cancel command button, if one exists.

- Press Alt+spacebar to open the dialog box's Control menu and choose Close.

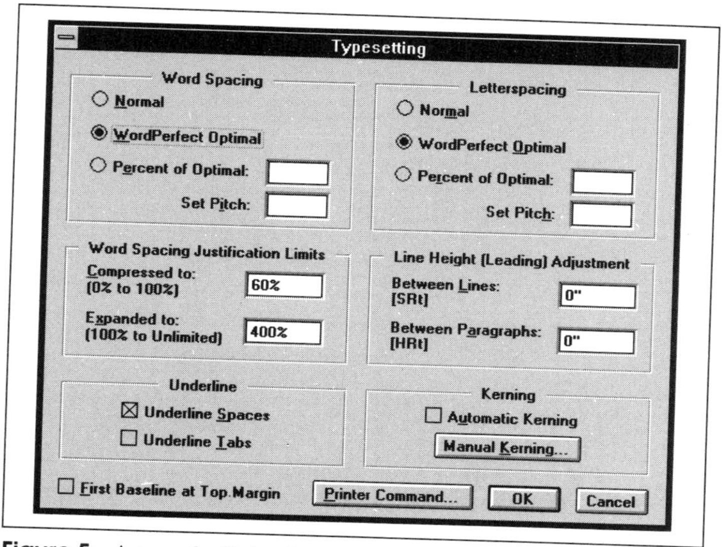

Figure 5: A sample dialog box

● NOTES

Dialog Box Elements: Table 5 shows examples of various elements available in dialog boxes, and summarizes mouse and keyboard techniques for using those elements.

When you've finished making choices from the dialog box, click the OK button, or tab to the OK button and press ↵.

Table 5: Dialog box elements

Symbol	Meaning
`·BMF`	**Text Box**: Click or tab to the text box, and start typing at the insertion point position. Use Backspace or Del to make corrections. In some cases, can use drop-down list boxes to choose text.
▲▼	**Scroll Bar**: Click the up or down arrow, or drag the scrolling box, or click anywhere in the scroll bar, or use the arrow, PgUp, and PgDn keys to scroll. Double-click the option you want, or move the highlight to the option you want and press ↵.
◉ ○	**Option Buttons** (also called radio buttons): Choose any one of the mutually exclusive buttons shown by clicking the option you want. Or tab to the button group, and then use the arrow keys to choose the button you want. A filled button indicates the selected option.
☒ ☐	**Check Boxes**: Choose (or "unchoose") each option you want. Or tab to the option you want and press the spacebar. Boxes containing an X are selected options.
⬙	**Drop-down List Box**: Click the arrow to open the list, use the scroll bar to scroll through the list, then click the option you want. Or tab to the option, press Alt+↓ to open the list, press the ↑ or ↓ keys to highlight the option you want, and then press Alt+↓ again to choose the option.

Table 5: Dialog box elements (continued)

Symbol	Meaning
⬍	**Scroll Arrows**: Click the Up button to increase, or Down arrow to decrease, the value in the accompanying box. Or tab to the option, type in a new value, or press ↑ or ↓ to increase or decrease the value shown.
OK / Cancel	**Command Buttons**: Click the button you want, or tab to the button you want and press ↵ or the spacebar. You can select the default button (with a darkened border) just by pressing ↵. If the button includes an underlined letter, hold down the Alt key and type the underlined letter to select that button.

Dialog Box Symbols: In addition to the command name, some command buttons will include special markings, as summarized in Table 6.

See Also   Menus, Windows

Table 6: Symbols used in dialog boxes

Symbol	Meaning
...(ellipsis)	Indicates that the command button opens another dialog box or lets you provide more information
>>	Expands the dialog box to show you some new options
Dimmed (grayed)	Indicates that the option is currently unavailable
Dark border	Indicates the default button, which is automatically selected if you press ↵

DISPLAY

The Display command enables you to change the appearance of text and graphics on your screen.

To Change the Screen Display

1. Choose File ➤ Preferences ➤ Display.

2. Choose one or more options and change settings as necessary (see Options).

3. Press ↵ or click OK when done.

● OPTIONS

Document Window Options

The following options are chosen when an "X" appears in their associated check boxes. Click on the check box to select and deselect an option.

Text in Windows System Colors	Displays text in Windows system colors instead of WordPerfect colors.
Graphics in Black & White	Displays graphics in black and white rather than the colors selected for the document window.
Auto Redisplay in Draft Mode	Reformats text after each editing change or when the Tab, Enter, ↑, or ↓ keys are pressed. Turn this option off to speed up editing; text will be reformatted when you scroll through it or when you press Ctrl+F3.

Display **C**olumns Side-by-Side	Displays columns side by side, just as they appear when printed. Turning this option off displays columns on separate pages to speed up scrolling. You can then see how the columns will look when printed by choosing **File ➤** Print Preview.
Display **M**erge Codes	Displays the field codes in merge documents.
Display **S**culptured Dialog Boxes	Creates a three-dimensional effect with dialog boxes but slightly slows the display.

Color Options

Draft Mode Colors	Choose this option to select the colors that will represent the appearance and size attributes of text while in the Draft Mode.
Reveal Codes Colors	Choose this option to change the colors of the text, codes, or cursor as displayed in the Reveal Codes window.

Other Options

Display **V**ertical/ **H**orizontal Scroll Bar	Click the check boxes to display either or both scroll bars.
Hard Return Character Display As	Lets you assign a character to follow hard returns, which are normally invisible in the document window. Move the insertion point to the Display As text box and enter the desired character. You can also assign a WordPerfect special character (Ctrl+W and select desired character). To make hard returns invisible again, just delete the character.

Units of Measure — Changes the default units of measure for the display and entry of numbers in dialog boxes and for the status bar display. Each option has a pop-up list from which to choose inches ("), inches (i), centimeters (c), points (p), or 1200ths of an inch (w).

● **NOTES** None of the screen display options affect printed output. Some of the display options lead to additional menus.

See Also Columns, Display Pitch, Document Comments, Document Window, Font Attributes, Menu Setup, Merge Operations, Print Preview, Rewrite, Special Characters, Windows

DISPLAY PITCH AND FONT ADJUSTMENT

The Display Pitch command controls the width of an on-screen character or space and normal mode on the Draft mode screen displays. Regardless of font size, WordPerfect always displays characters the same size on the Draft mode screen. Although text will usually wrap properly, exceptions occur when WordPerfect encounters codes that call for an absolute measurement (such as tabs, indents, table margins, and column margins). In these cases, WordPerfect uses the display pitch to determine the width of one on-screen character or space.

To Change the Display Pitch and Font Adjustment

1. Choose Layout ➤ Document ➤ Display Pitch (Ctrl+Shift+F9, D).

2. In normal mode, to adjust the width of characters displayed, under Display Font Adjustment, click **Auto**

(default) for automatic font adjustment or **Manual** to set adjustment to some percentage of normal (default is 100 percent).

3. In Draft mode, to adjust the width of characters displayed, click **Auto** (default) to use WordPerfect's automatic display pitch width, or **Manual** to set a pitch of your own (the default is 0.1 inch).

4. If you chose Manual, enter a display-pitch width in inches.

5. Press ↵ or click OK when done.

• NOTES Changing the display pitch can make columns and tables more legible. If column text overlaps, try decreasing the display pitch to increase the amount of space between columns. If the columns are too far apart, try increasing the display pitch. Changes to display pitch affect the Draft mode screen of the current document only. Changes in the Font Adjustment affect the normal mode screen.

If the Draft mode display pitch setting is 0.1 inch, a 1-inch indent is as wide as 10 characters or spaces (10×0.1 inch = 1 inch).

See Also Display, Draft Mode

DOCUMENT COMMENTS

The Comment command enables you to insert nonprinting comments into a document and convert existing comments to text.

To Create a Comment

1. Move the insertion point to the location where the comment should begin.

2. Choose **Tools ➤ Comment ➤ Create**.

3. Type the comment. The comment can include different type styles (**B**old, **U**nderline, or **I**talic) as desired.

4. Press ↵ or click OK when done.

To Create a Comment from Existing Text

1.   Select the text using the mouse or keyboard.

2.   Choose Tools ➤ Comment ➤ Create. The selected text will become a comment.

To Edit a Comment

1.   Move the insertion point to the location just after the comment you want to edit.

2.   Choose Tools ➤ Comment ➤ Edit.

3.   Edit the comment.

4.   Press ↵ or click OK when done.

To Convert a Comment to Text

1.   Move the insertion point to the location just after the comment you want to convert.

2.   Choose Tools ➤ Comment ➤ Convert to Text. The comment will be inserted into the document text.

To Delete a Comment

To delete a comment, turn on Reveal Codes and delete the comment code [Comment]. You can also convert the comment to text and delete the text.

● **NOTES**   Comments display on the document window in a double-lined box, unless you turn the comments display off, or the comments are within a column. Comments never print on the document itself, unless you first convert them to text.

You can add bold, underlining, or italics to comments.

See Also   Delete Operations, Display, Reveal Codes, Selecting Text

DOCUMENT COMPARE

The Document Compare command lets you compare two revisions of the same document and mark changes in one of them.

To Compare Two Documents

The current document is compared to a version of the same document that is stored on disk. WordPerfect marks phrases in the current document that differ from the stored version. To compare to documents:

1. Choose **Tools ➤** Doc**u**ment Compare ➤ **A**dd Markings.

2. Enter the name of the document to compare the current document with. If you saved the current document, its name will appear in the text box.

3. Choose **C**ompare.

The differences between the two documents will be marked in the current document. Redline and strikeout codes are inserted into the document surrounding the changed phrases. Deleted phrases appear with a line drawn through the text. Added phrases appear in red, if you have a color monitor. Moved phrases are surrounded by notices following (and preceding) the text that was moved.

To remove the marks from the current document, either:

- Choose **Tools ➤** Document Compare ➤ **R**emove Markings.
- Choose **E**dit ➤ **U**ndo immediately after you compare the documents.

● **NOTES**   Be sure to make backup copies of the documents before starting the comparison since the operation is complex.

Document Compare tests for differences phrase-by-phrase, not word-by-word. Phrases are defined as text between punctuation marks, hard return or hard page codes, footnote and endnote codes, and the end of the text. The comparison includes footnotes, endnotes, and tables but not the text inside graphics boxes, headers or footers.

You can change the appearance of the strikeout and redline text in the printed copy by choosing File ➤ Preferences ➤ Print. Choose one of the Redline Methods: **P**rinter Dependent, **M**ark Left Margin, or Mark **A**lternating Margins. You can also change the redline character by entering the desired character in the text box (not available with the Printer Dependent choice).

See Also   Redline Method

DOCUMENT SUMMARY

You can define document management and summary information for the current document or as a default for all documents created during an editing session. Document summary features let you organize documents, assign meaningful document names to them, and assign a document type that can be used to categorize documents.

To Create or Edit a Summary

1. From anywhere in the document, choose Layout ➤ Document ➤ Summary (Ctrl+Shift+F9,S).

2. Choose one or more options and enter values for them (see Options).

3. Press ↵ or click OK when done.

To Set Default Summary Entries

To set a default Descriptive Type, to change the subject search string to one other than "RE:" and to be prompted to create a summary each time you save a document:

1. Choose File ➤ Preferences ➤ Document Summary.

2. Choose one or more options and enter values for them.

3.   Press ↵ or click OK when done.

● OPTIONS

Entries for Defining Summaries

Descriptive Name   Enter up to 68 characters. The name can appear in the File Manager Viewer.

Descriptive Type   Enter a category (such as "Memos") of up to 20 characters by which the File Manager may sort.

Creation Date   The date of the original document summary is provided by the system and remains unchanged unless you change it. The revision date is updated by the system each time the document is saved; it cannot be changed.

Author and Typist   Type author's and typist's names (up to 60 characters each) or choose Extract to enter the author and typist of the last document in this session.

Subject   Choose Extract, and WordPerfect for Windows will use as the subject text the first 160 characters that follow *RE:* in your document. (This heading can be part of the document's text; it does not need to be coded in any special manner.) You can also tell Extract to search for a different heading (of up to 39 characters).

     Choose File ➤ Preferences ➤ Document Summary and edit the Subject Search Text. To specify a different subject, type up to 160 characters in the Subject box after choosing Layout ➤ Document ➤ Summary.

Account	Enter up to 160 to identify the document by account name (e.g., customer, client, project).
Keywords	Enter one or more keywords to help you define the document, separated by commas, up to a total of 160 characters.
Abstract	Enter up to 780 characters, or choose Extract to automatically enter the first 400 characters of this document. Entering a hard return will remove the Document Summary dialog box from the screen.

Using Extract to Define Summary

Choosing Extract and then Yes from the Document Summary dialog box provides a shortcut to defining a document summary. It will enter the names of the author and typist of the last document edited during this session, the first 150 characters after the Subject Search Heading, and the first 400 characters of this document. You may then edit any of the extracted entries.

Other Document Summary Operations

In addition to Extract described above, the other available operations are:

Save As	Click Save As and enter a file name for the saved summary.
Print	Click Print to print the summary.
Delete	Click Delete or press ↵ while the Delete button is selected, and then choose Yes to delete the current document summary.

● **NOTES**   After defining summaries, you can use the File Manager to search for documents based on summary information.

See Also   Exit, File Manager, Preferences, Save/Save As

DOCUMENT WINDOW

The document window, shown in Figure 6, is your home base for most editing operations. You'll see this screen when you first start WordPerfect, and whenever you edit text and graphics. The document window starts out nearly blank, except for the document title in the window title bar, the insertion point and the status line. As you work on the document, WordPerfect will automatically format it to look as much like the final printed result as possible. Word-Perfect offers an optional simplified draft mode that lets you focus just on your text.

The *insertion point* indicates where the next character that you type will appear. You can either type characters at the insertion point, or you can move the insertion point without actually typing anything.

The *status line* at the bottom right corner of the document window indicates the position of the insertion point on the screen in relation

Figure 6:   A WordPerfect document window

to its position on a printed sheet of paper. The status line never prints on your documents. The usual status line indicators include:

Font   Shows the font attribute of the current character (e.g., Courier 10cpi)

Pg   Shows which page you are editing (e.g., Pg 2)

Ln   Shows which line you are currently editing, as measured from the top of the printed page (e.g., Ln 1")

Pos   Shows the insertion point position, as measured from the left of the printed page (e.g, Pos 1.67")

You can also elect to have a Button Bar and a ruler displayed on the screen in addition to the standard document window menu.

Document Window Manipulation   The window can be maximized to fill the screen, minimized to an icon, or restored from a full screen or an icon to its original size. You can have several document windows on the screen at a time, with only one active. The active document window will be in the foreground with its title bar darkened. You can switch from one window to another by clicking on the title bar or choosing the document window name from the Window menu.

To open a document window, choose File ➤ Open (F4) and select a file name. To close the active document window, choose File ➤ Close (Ctrl+F4).

Arranging Document Windows   If you have several documents open, you can arrange their windows in two different ways: Cascade or Tile. Cascaded windows overlap while Tiled windows are arranged with no overlap. Choose Window ➤ Cascade or Window ➤ Tile.

Many WordPerfect features temporarily cover the document window to show you menus, dialog boxes, and other editing or viewing screens.

Most formatting features insert special codes into your document. These codes are invisible on the document window. Choose View ➤ Reveal Codes (Alt+F3) to display these codes in the lower portion of the window. The Reveal Codes window can be sized by dragging the separating line up or down.

See Also   Delete, Draft Mode, Insert, Print Preview, Reveal Codes, Typeover

DOS

The Windows Program Manager lets you run one or more DOS commands or programs without first exiting WordPerfect.

1. Minimize WordPerfect by clicking the Minimize button in the upper right corner.

2. Double-click the DOS icon in the Windows Main group of the Program Manager.

This method lets you run as many commands and programs as you want. Type **EXIT** and press ↵ to return to the Program Manager.

DRAFT MODE

The Draft Mode document window lets you focus just on your text. It displays text in plain monospace, and any graphics appear only as box outlines. The advantage of Draft mode is that screen operations occur faster than in the standard document window.

To Switch to and from Draft Mode

1. Choose View ➤ Draft Mode.

2. To switch back to the Normal Edit mode, repeat step 1 to deselect Draft mode.

● **NOTES**   You can set the draft mode display colors through the Display Settings dialog box. Choose File ➤ Preferences ➤ Display, click the Draft Mode Colors button, and select the desired color attributes from the palette.

See Also Display

ENVIRONMENT

You can customize WordPerfect for your hardware setup and work preferences. All choices are made by clicking check boxes in the Environment Settings dialog box. Environment options are typically set only once and affect all new WordPerfect documents.

To Change the Setup Options

1. Choose File ➤ Preferences ➤ Environment.

2. Choose one or more environment options and respond to any additional prompts (see Options).

3. Press ↵ or click OK when done.

● **OPTIONS** The Environment Settings dialog box is composed of six sections.

Settings The options in this section enable the use of several of WordPerfect's automatic functions.

Auto Code Placement	Inserts margin and justification codes at the beginning of the current paragraph or page rather than at the insertion point (see the Auto Code Placement command reference).
Confirm on Code Deletion	Prompts you to confirm the deletion if you attempt to delete a code when the Reveal Codes option is turned off.

Fast Save	Saves the document with all formatting except print formatting. While this option speeds the saving of files, it slows the print out of those files.
Allow Undo	Enables the Undo capability in the Edit menu (see the Undo command reference).
Format Retrieved Documents for Default Printer	Formats any retrieved document for the default printer. If the document was saved with formatting specific to another printer, some fonts and other print attributes may look different.

Beep On   The options in this section control when the computer's beep will sound: in case of an Error; in case of a Hyphenation question (when Hyphenation is on); or in case of a Search Failure.

Menu   The options in this section determine the appearance of the pull-down menus. Select Display Shortcut Keys to display keyboard alternatives alongside the command names on the menus. Select Display Last Open Filenames to display the names of the last four opened files at the bottom of the File menu for quick retrieval. You can retrieve one of these files by clicking its name.

Ruler   The options in this section determine the look and function of the various elements on the ruler.

Tabs Snap to Ruler Grid	Automatically moves a tab to the nearest invisible ruler grid line; grid lines are spaced every $\frac{1}{16}$ inch
Show Ruler Guides	Displays a dotted vertical line down through your document when you drag a margin or tab marker

| Ruler **B**uttons on Top | Displays the ruler buttons above the ruler distance marks and tab indicators |
| Automatic Ruler **D**isplay | Displays the ruler in all open documents. |

Prompt for Hyphenation   The radio buttons in this area determine when WordPerfect will ask you for assistance in hyphenating words: **N**ever, **W**hen Required, or **A**lways.

Hyphenation   The radio buttons in this area determine whether WordPerfect will use the **E**xternal or **I**nternal hyphenation dictionary (see the Hyphenation command reference).

See Also   Backup, Document Summary, Hyphenation, Preferences, Units of Measure

EQUATIONS

The Equation Editor lets you create, edit, and align mathematical and scientific equations.

To Create or Edit an Equation

1.   With the insertion point at the intended location of the equation, choose **G**raphics ➤ **E**quation ➤ **C**reate (or **E**dit).

2.   Type the equation or select elements from the equation palette (see Notes).

3.   To see how it will look when printed, choose **V**iew ➤ **R**edisplay (Ctrl+F3).

4.   If desired, change the equation settings (see Notes).

5.   Choose **F**ile ➤ **C**lose (Ctrl+F4) or click the Close button to return to your document window.

To Define Default Settings for Equations

1. From the document window, choose **File** ➤ Preferences ➤ Equations.

2. Choose one or more of the equations options (see Notes).

3. Click OK.

To Change Equation Settings for a Single Equation

1. From the Equation Editor window, choose **File** ➤ Settings (or click the Settings button).

2. Choose one or more of the equations options (see Notes).

3. Click OK.

To Delete an Equation Box

From the document window, set Reveal Codes on and delete the [Equ Box:] code.

● **NOTES** The Equation Editor lets you edit and select print options for equations with all the special symbols and typesetting standards. However, it does not solve the equations for you.

Equations can be stored in one of five types of graphics boxes (see the Graphics and Graphic Boxes reference), although Equation boxes are easiest to use.

Typing Equations The Equation Editor window has three panes: the top Editing Pane, used to create and edit equations; the bottom Display Pane, for the graphical display of the equation; the Equation Palette on the left, with commands, symbols, and functions you may insert into the equation.

The basic techniques for editing equations are the same as those for editing text, although you must use special commands (listed below) to print spaces and line breaks. The building blocks of equations are symbols, numbers, variables, and commands. Use spaces to separate these elements from one another.

Symbols can be keyboard symbols, symbols from WordPerfect character sets, or symbols chosen from the Equation Palette.

Variables include any alphabetic characters that aren't recognized as reserved commands. Variables must begin with alphabetic characters, can be one or more characters long, and can contain numbers.

Numbers are any nonnegative integers (e.g., 0, 1, 32767). To enter a real number (including negative and decimal numbers), surround the number with braces, as in {-3.24}.

Commands all have some formatting function, such as drawing a line, creating a matrix, or arranging variables in an equation. You can type them in upper- or lowercase, or choose them from the Equation Palette. Table 7 lists some common equation commands.

Table 7: Equation Commands

Command	Description
ALIGNC	Center-aligns a *variable* over a line or in a matrix
ALIGNL	Left-aligns a *variable* over a line or in a matrix
ALIGNR	Right-aligns a *variable* over a line or in a matrix
BINOM	Creates a binomial construction from two *variables* that follow
BINOMSM	Creates a binomial construction from two *variables* that follow, but in the next smaller font (printer- and font-dependent)
BOLD	Boldfaces the *variable*, symbol, or function that follows
FROM	Provides beginning and ending limits for a symbol, and must be used in conjunction with the TO command
FUNC	Treats a *variable* name as a mathematical function so that it will not be printed in italics

Table 7: Equation Commands (continued)

Command	Description
HORZ	Specifies a distance to move horizontally, in increments that are a percentage of the current font size (for example, *HORZ 100* moves the cursor 12 points to the right if you're using a 12-point font; *HORZ –100* moves the cursor 12 points to the left for a 12-point font)
ITAL	Italicizes a *variable,* symbol, or function
LEFT	Defines a delimiter that will expand to the size of the subgroup it encloses; if LEFT is used in an equation, RIGHT must also be used, but you don't have to use identical (or matched) left and right delimiter symbols
MATFORM	Used with MATRIX to align *variables,* where ALIGNC, ALIGNL, and ALIGNR specify the alignment, *&* separates columns, and # separates rows
MATRIX	Creates a matrix of *variables,* where *&* separates columns and # separates rows (think of *&* as meaning "and" and # as meaning "over," e.g., *x & y # a & b* means "x and y over a and b")
NROOT	Creates the *n*th root sign over a *variable,* such as *NROOT 3 {x+y}* (the cube root of x + y).
OVER	Creates a fraction by placing one *variable* over a second *variable*
OVERLINE	Places a line over a *variable*
OVERSM	Same as OVER, but reduces the entire construction to the next smaller available font (printer- and font-dependent)
PHANTOM	Occupies the same space as the *variable* that follows, but displays only blank space; useful for lining up stacked equations

Table 7: Equation Commands (continued)

Command	Description
RIGHT	Used in conjunction with LEFT to display the right delimiter (*see* LEFT)
SQRT	Places a square-root radical over *variable*
STACK	Stacks equations; # is used to start a new line for *variables* that appear on separate rows
STACKALIGN	Stacks *variables* on specified characters; & precedes the character used for alignment in each row and # separates the rows
SUB *or* _	Changes into a subscript the *variable* to its right
SUP *or* ^	Changes into a superscript the *variable* to its right
TO	Used in conjunction with FROM to set starting and ending limits for a symbol
UNDERLINE	Places a bar under the *variable*
VERT	Like HORZ, but moves the cursor vertically in increments that are a percentage of the current point size
{ *and* }	Delineates a group
~	Inserts a full space
~g	Inserts a quarter space
&	Used with the MATRIX and MATFORM commands to delineate columns; used with STACKALIGN to indicate the alignment character
#	Used with MATRIX, STACK, and STACKALIGN to delineate rows
.	Used with LEFT and RIGHT to display an invisible delimiter
\	Prints a command literally; for example, *THETA* alone displays the Greek letter theta (θ), but *\THETA* displays the word *THETA*

To change the contents of the Equation Palette from commands to other selections, such as symbols, Greek letters, trigonometric functions, or arrows, click the drop-down menu at the top of the palette and highlight another list.

Editing Pane Commands   You can choose these commands by clicking a button in the Editing Pane Button Bar:

Retrieve	Retrieves an equation that has been saved as a file.
Redisplay	Displays the current equation graphically in the Display Pane without leaving the Editing Window.
Cut, Copy, and Paste	Perform Clipboard operations.
Zoom 200% and Zoom Fill	Shrink or enlarge the image of the equation in the Display Pane.
Settings	Lets you change equation alignment within the graphics box and control certain printing options. Click OK when done. (See Equation Settings below.)
EquPos	Lets you choose the box type, determine the box size, adjust the equation within the box, choose to wrap text around the box, or anchor the box to a specific character, paragraph, or page. Click OK when done.

The Equation Editor File menu also lets you save and retrieve equation box files. Use the Graphics ➤ Equation menu to renumber, caption, or position an equation box.

Equation Settings   These settings control the appearance of the equation, and are available for the current equation, or as initial settings for all equations.

Print as **G**raphics

Click the check box to print equations as graphics (default), or leave blank to print them in the current base font, using graphics characters only if a symbol does exist in the printer font.

Graphic Font Size

(Applicable only when Print as **G**raphics is set on). Choose **D**efault Font to use either the font size of the initial base font (if there are no Equation Box Options codes before the equation), or the font size prior to an Equation Box Options code [Equ Opt]. Or choose **P**oint Size and enter your own point size.

Horizontal Alignment

Enables you to align the equation horizontally at the **L**eft edge, **C**enter, or **R**ight edge of the graphics box.

Vertical Alignment

Enables you to align the equation vertically at the **T**op edge, **C**enter, or **B**ottom edge of the graphics box.

Keyboard

Displays the currently selected keyboard for editing equations. To select a new keyboard, choose File ➤ Preferences ➤**K**eyboard.

● **EXAMPLE** The following commands entered into the Equation Editor will yield the equations shown in Figure 7.

SQRT {a^2 + b^2} OVER {x_1 - y_1}
SUM FROM {x=0} TO INF
tan THETA = {sin THETA} OVER {cos THETA}

See Also Button Bar, Graphics and Graphic Boxes, Special Characters

Equation typed as...	Appears as...
SQRT {a^2 + b^2} OVER {x_1 - y_1}	$\dfrac{\sqrt{a^2+b^2}}{x_1-y_1}$
SUM FROM {x=0} TO INF	$\displaystyle\sum_{x=0}^{-}$
tan THETA = {sin THETA} OVER {cos THETA}	$\tan\theta = \dfrac{\sin\theta}{\cos\theta}$

Figure 7: Sample Equations

EXIT

Use the features of the Exit command to save any changes to the document and leave WordPerfect.

To Exit WordPerfect

1. Choose File ➤ Exit (Alt+F4).

2. If you have made changes to any open document, a prompt is displayed: *Save changes to <filename>?* Choose **Yes** to save, **No** to exit without saving the current file, or Cancel to abandon the operation.

3. If the file has yet to be saved, the Save **As** dialog box is displayed. Enter a file name and choose **Save**.

● **NOTES**   Always exit from the document window *before* turning off the computer.

If you have multiple documents open, you will be prompted to save each document that has been modified since last saved.

See Also   Cancel, Document Summary, Document Window, Environment, File Manager, Master Document, Save Document

FILE MANAGER

The File Manager provides many advanced file manipulation features, enabling you to:

- navigate through drives, directories, subdirectories, and files

- manipulate and edit files

- search for word patterns or files in any window

- view file lists sorted by path, file name, extension, size, date/time, descriptive name, or type

- create directories, change the current directory, and print a directory listing

- display and print information about the system, windows, printer, or disks

- add applications

- arrange windows and icons and select the active window

To Access the File Manager

1.   Choose File ➤ File Manager.

2.   Choose an operation from the menu bar or Button Bar (see Options).

3.   Double-click the Control-menu box when done.

• NOTES   When you first choose File Manager, the Navigator window shows the available drives. Select one of the drives by double-clicking. The directories on the drive are listed in the next pane.

• OPTIONS

File Manager Menu

Menu	Functions
File	To open, retrieve, or print a file using an associated application; print the contents of a window; Run DOS or Windows executable files, commands, or batch files; delete, copy, move, or rename a file or directory; change file attributes; change or create a directory; set or change file preferences (either in current environment or an associate) or setup printer; exit the File Manager
Edit	To select or unselect all text in active window, copy or append text to the Clipboard
Search	To find word patterns in selected files or windows; search for the next or previous occurrence of the string; find files using a file template (wildcards)
View	To create windows and set up display operations; select the view layout options; display a file list window or Navigator window; display a File Viewer window; display or edit a Quick List; show and setup the Button Bar; set screen fonts; set the window display options (such as sort order and list specifications)
Info	To display and print information about the system, windows, printer, disks
Applications	To run applications (such as Thesaurus or Speller) and assign them to a menu
Window	To arrange windows and icons, select the active window, and close the windows

File Manager Button Bar   The File Manager's Button Bar contains frequently used menu options. To turn the Button Bar on, choose File ➤ File Manager ➤ View ➤ Button Bar. To change the buttons in the bar:

1. Choose File ➤ File Manager ➤ View ➤ Button Bar Setup ➤ Edit.

2. Choose the menu selections for which you want to create buttons. The buttons will automatically appear on the Button Bar.

3. Click OK or press ↵ when done.

To change the position of a button, drag it to its new location. To remove a button from the bar, drag it off the bar.

See Also   Button Bar, Document Summary, Password, Print, Retrieve, Save, Search

FLUSH RIGHT

This command aligns text flush against the right margin. The Flush Right command is useful for single-line entries, including dates, business headings and addresses, lists, and headers or footers on right-facing pages.

To Right-Align One Line of Text

1. Position the insertion point at the location where you want to right-align new text, or to the left of existing text.

2. Choose Layout ➤ Line ➤ Flush Right (Alt+F7).

3. If you want dot leaders, repeat step 2.

4. If you are right-aligning new text, type the new text and press ↵.

To Right-Align Several Existing Lines

1. Select the text you want to right-align.

2. Choose Layout ➤ Line ➤ Flush Right (Alt+F7).

To Right-Align Large Areas of Text

1. Position the insertion point above the text to be right-aligned.

2. Choose Layout ➤ Justification ➤ Right (Ctrl+R). The text will right-align to the end of the document or the next justification code.

● **NOTES**   To remove the right justification, remove the [Just:Right] code from the Reveal Codes window.

See Also   Justification, Selecting Text, Tabs

FONT

You can change the font (typeface and point size) anywhere in your document and set the initial font for selected text, for the current document, and for all documents.

To Change Fonts Anywhere in a Document

1. Position the insertion point where you want the new font to take effect, or select existing text.

2. Choose View ➤ Ruler (Alt+Shift+F3) to display the ruler, if it is not already displayed.

Then…

3. Click the Font button.

4. Choose the desired font in the list.

Or…

3. Double-click the Font button.

4. Highlight the font you want.

5. Select the point size (scalable fonts only).

6. Click the check boxes of the other text attributes you want.

7. Click OK or press ↵ to return to the document window.

You can also choose Font ➤ Font (F9) to reach the same Font dialog box and proceed as in steps 4–7 above.

● **NOTES**   Footnotes, endnotes, equations, and graphics box cap-tions use the *document initial font* unless you insert an Options code for these items.

To Set the Printer Initial Font

The printer initial font automatically becomes the initial font for all documents, unless you override it.

1. If you are using Windows printer drivers, choose File ➤ Select Printer ➤ Initial Font. If you are using WordPerfect printer drivers, select File ➤ Select Printer ➤ Setup➤ Initial Font.

2. Choose a font as described in "To Change Fonts Anywhere in a Document" above.

3. To return to your document, click OK in the Printer Initial Font dialog box, and then Select in the Select Printer dialog box.

To Set the Document Initial Font

The document initial font affects the current document only, over-riding the printer's initial font.

1. Choose Layout ➤ Document ➤ Initial Font (Ctrl+Shift+F9,F).

2. Choose a font as in steps 4–5 above.

3. To return to your document, click OK in the Document Initial Font dialog box.

To Add Fonts to the Ruler List

To assign a font to the list displayed by clicking the Ruler Font button:

1. Access the Font dialog box, as outlined above.

2. Click the Assign to Ruler button.

3. You will see the Ruler Fonts Menu dialog box. Select a font from the Font List box.

4. Click the Add button to add the font to the Fonts on Ruler list.

5. Repeat steps 3 and 4 if you want to add other fonts.

6. Click OK twice to return to the document window.

See Also   Cartridges and Fonts, Font Attributes, Footnotes and Endnotes, Graphics and Graphic Boxes, Printer Select, Selecting Text

FONT ATTRIBUTES

With the Font Attributes command, you can change the appearance, size, and color of the currently chosen font.

To Set a Font Attribute in New Text

1. Position the insertion point at the location where you want the new attribute to begin.

2. Double-click the Ruler Font button (or choose Font).

3. Choose a font attribute (see Notes).

4. Make additional choices as needed (if you chose Color or Size).

5. Repeat steps 2–4 as needed to set additional font attributes.

6. Click OK to return to the document window.

7. Type your text.

8. Return the font attributes to normal by choosing Font ➤ Normal (Ctrl+N).

To Set a Font Attribute in Existing Text

1. Select the text whose font attribute you want to change.

2. Access the Font dialog box through the Font menu, as described above.

3. Choose a font attribute (see Notes).

4. Repeat steps 1–3 as needed to set additional font attributes.

● **NOTES**   The font attributes are all variations of the current font. Most attributes can be set either through the Font dialog box or the Font menu. Some exceptions are noted below.

The final appearance of printed text depends on the printer selection and font. The *on-screen* display of fonts depends on the type of monitor you have and the screen display settings. Print the Word-Perfect PRINTER.TST file to see how the font attributes look with your printer.

Font Attributes   You can choose from among these font attributes: Color, Normal (Ctrl+N), Bold (Ctrl+B), Italic (Ctrl+I), Underline (Ctrl+U), Double Underline, Redline, Strikeout, Subscript, Superscript, Outline, Shadow, Small Cap, and Size. Color and Normal are available only through the Font menu. Outline, Shadow, and Small Cap are available only through the Font dialog box. The keyboard shortcuts shown in parentheses can replace steps 2 and 3 above.

The Color option changes the color of printed text. (Of course, this option only works with color printers.) A variable color spectrum shows how the different percentages of red, green, and blue that compose standard print colors will appear with respect to Hue, Saturation, and Lumination. You can also choose a predefined color from the pull-down menu (**Custom**, **B**lack, **W**hite, **R**ed, **Gr**een, **B**lue, **Y**ellow, **M**agenta, C**y**an, **O**range, **G**ray, Brow**n**). Click OK or press ⏎ when done.

The **N**ormal option turns off all attributes, returning text to the un-adorned current font.

The **S**ize option lets you choose **F**ine, **S**mall, **L**arge, **V**ery Large, or **E**xtra Large.

To Choose a Print Size Ratio

1. Select File ➤ Preferences ➤ Print.

2. Enter the Size Attribute Ratios in the Print Settings dialog box, relative to the base font, for fine, small, large, very large, extra large, superscript, and subscript text.

3. Click OK or press ⏎.

The relative size of the Size options depends on the ratios you set. Your printer must be able to scale the fonts accordingly for these ratios to have a significant effect. Run PRINTER.TST if you have any doubt.

See Also Display, Document Compare, Font, Printer Select, Redlining and Strikeout, Selecting Text

FOOTNOTES AND ENDNOTES

You can use footnotes or endnotes to list sources or provide more detailed information on an item in your text. Footnotes print at the bottom of the page where they are referenced. Endnotes are usually placed at the end of the document. Because footnote and endnote commands work almost identically, we'll just refer to them as *notes*.

To Create a Note

1. Position the insertion point to the right of the text to be marked with a note number.

2. Choose Layout ➤ Footnote or Endnote ➤ Create.

3. Type the text of your note.

4. Choose Close when done.

To Edit a Note

1. Choose Layout ➤ Footnote or Endnote ➤ Edit.

2. Enter the number, character, or letter of the note you want to edit. Then click OK or press ↵.

3. Edit the note.

4. Choose Close when done.

To Renumber Notes

1. Position the insertion point at the location where the renumbering should begin.

2. Choose Layout ➤ Footnote or Endnote ➤ New Number.

3. Enter the starting number in the New Number text box (using the current note numbering method—number, letter, or character), and click OK or press ↵.

To Set Note Options

1. Position the insertion point at the location where the options should begin to take effect.

2. Choose Layout ➤ Footnote or Endnote ➤ Options.

3. Choose one or more options (see Options).

4. Click OK when done.

To Change Endnote Placement

1. Position the insertion point at the location where the endnotes should print (perhaps at the end of a chapter).

2. Choose Layout ➤ Page ➤ Page Break (Ctrl+↵) if you want a page break before the endnotes.

3. Choose Layout ➤ Endnote ➤ Placement.

4. Choose Yes to renumber any remaining notes, or No to continue from the current number.

To Delete a Note

• Select the note reference number in the document window and choose Edit ➤ Cut (Shift+Del).

• Choose View ➤ Reveal Codes (Alt+F3) and delete the [Footnote:] or [Endnote:] code.

• Place the insertion point before the note number and press the Delete key.

The notes below the deleted note will be renumbered automatically.

• **NOTES** WordPerfect automatically numbers and formats notes, and places them in your document.

When you create a note, the note number will automatically appear.

Notes may include normal editing and formatting features (e.g., Indent, Bold, Format, Center). Each note can contain approximately 65,000 characters.

Notes in Master Documents are numbered as if you were using one large document.

Graphics boxes in notes must use a character anchor type.

Endnotes Endnotes are grouped at the end of a document, unless you change endnote placement. You can choose Tools ➤ Generate (Alt+F12) to see how much space the endnotes will occupy, though this is not required to print endnotes.

Choose Layout ➤ Page ➤ Page Break or press Ctrl+↵ at the end of the document if you want endnotes to start on a new page.

● **OPTIONS**   You can choose one or more note options from the Footnote or Endnote Options dialog box (only the first 6 below are available for endnotes). These can be set for each document or, by using Initial Codes, set for all documents.

Line Spacing in Notes	Enter the line spacing for the notes (e.g., 1 for single-spaced).
Spacing **Between** Notes	Enter a measurement for amount of blank space between notes.
Minimum Note **Height**	Enter a measurement for the amount of text that should stay together if the note must be split across pages (the default is 0.5 inch).
Style in **Text**	Allows you to modify the default style of note numbers in text. A button on the right allows you to select font attributes, and you can add text or spaces to precede or follow the number.
Style in **Note**	Allows you to modify the default style of note numbers in the note. A button on the right allows you to select font attributes, and you can add text to precede or follow the note.
Numbering Method	Choose **Numbers**, **Letters**, or **Characters**. For **Characters**, enter up to 5 characters (e.g., ***+!**) without spaces between. After using each character, WordPerfect will recycle them by doubling (e.g., ******), tripling, and so on, up to 15 repetitions.

Restart Numbering on Each **P**age	Click the check box to restart numbers on each page, or leave it blank to number continuously throughout the document.
Separator	Choose **No** Line, 2-Inch line, or **M**argin to Margin to define the separation between text and footnotes.
Print (Continued…) **M**essage	Click the check box to print "continued" messages for footnotes that split across pages, or leave it blank to suppress messages.
Position	Choose **B**ottom of Page to always place footnotes at the bottom of the page (even when a page isn't full), or **A**fter Text to place footnotes just below the last line of text on a page.

See Also   Generate, Graphics and Graphic Boxes, Master Document

GENERATE

The Generate command compiles tables of contents, tables of authorities, indexes, lists, and cross-references in the current document and updates the amount of space required for endnotes.

To Generate Reference
Tables, Indexes, and Lists

1.   Choose **T**ools ➤ **G**enerate (Alt+F12).

2.   Choose **Y**es.

● **NOTES** Issuing the Generate command is the final step in creating tables of contents, tables of authorities, indexes, lists, cross-references, and endnotes, and will replace any existing entries.

You can issue the Generate command as often as you want and must do so after marking new list items, if you want them to appear in your final document.

You can edit generated entries; however, your editing will be lost when you regenerate the list.

See Also Cross-Reference, Footnotes and Endnotes, Index, Lists, Master Document, Table of Authorities, Table of Contents

GO TO

The Go To command lets you quickly move to a specific position in the document, a specific newspaper or parallel column, or a position within selected text.

To Move to a Specific Page or Location

1. Choose Edit ➤ Go To (Ctrl+G).

2. Enter a page number or choose an option to specify the destination location. Table 8 lists the destinations you can specify for regular text, selected text, and columns.

3. Click OK to move to the new location.

See Also Columns, Insertion Point, Selecting Text

Table 8: The Go To command options for normal, columnar, and selected text

Option	Normal Text	Columns	Selected Text
Go to Page Number	X	X	X
Top of Current Page	X		X
Bottom of Current Page	X		X
Top of Column		X	
Bottom of Column		X	
Previous Column		X	
Next Column		X	
First Column		X	
Last Column		X	
Beginning of Selection			X
Reselect Text			X

GRAPHICS AND GRAPHIC BOXES

WordPerfect lets you incorporate graphic images (as well as tables, equations, and other elements that are not simply "running text")

into a document and manipulate their size, placement, and other characteristics. You can add or delete captions, determine whether text wraps around a box or is superimposed over it, and "anchor" the text to a particular character, paragraph, or page. These operations involve the use of a *graphics box*, a rectangular area that you set aside in your document to hold the image. WordPerfect has five types of graphics boxes: Figure, Text, Table, Equation, and User. This entry discusses operations you can perform on Figure boxes; see the entries for Equations, Tables, and Text Boxes for information on those box types. See the Border Options entry for the different border styles available for all box types.

To Add Graphics to a Document

You can create a graphics box and insert an image into it at the same time:

1. Position the insertion point at the location where the figure is to appear.
2. Choose Graphics ➤ Figure ➤ Create.
3. Choose File ➤ Retrieve.
4. In the Retrieve Figure dialog box, select or enter the graphics file name.
5. Choose Retrieve.
6. Choose File ➤ Close (or Ctrl+F4) to return to your document.

For figure boxes, you can also follow this shortcut:

1. Position the insertion point at the location where the figure is to appear.
2. Choose Graphics ➤ Figure ➤ Retrieve (F11).
3. Double-click on the desired graphics file name.

To insert an image from a graphics file into another type of box, use the box editor menu selections.

To Create Other Box Types

You can create other types of boxes with the Graphics menu: text boxes to set text apart from the body of the document; equation boxes for mathematical expressions; table boxes for numerical or statistical data and maps; and user boxes for anything else. To create a new box:

1. Position the insertion point where the box is to appear.

2. Choose **Graphics** ➤ *box type* ➤ **Create**. Box types include Text **B**ox (Alt+F11), **E**quation, **T**able Box, or **U**ser Box.

3. For a Table or User box, select the appropriate editor and choose OK.

4. Enter the table text or an equation in the box.

5. Choose **File** ➤ **Close** to return to the document window.

You can also retrieve existing text or equations into the box through the box editor:

1. Create the box as outlined above.

2. Choose **File** ➤ **Retrieve**.

3. Select or type a file name in the text box.

4. Choose **Retrieve**.

5. Choose **File** ➤ **Close** to return to the document window.

To Edit a Figure Box

You can open the appropriate box editor by double-clicking in the box or by using the menu system.

WordPerfect has three box editors: Figure Editor, Equation Editor, and Text Editor. This section discusses the Figure Editor; see Equations and Text Boxes for details of the others.

1. Choose **Graphics** ➤ **Figure** ➤ **Edit**, or press Shift+F11.

2. Enter the figure number and click OK.

3. Use the Figure Editor to make changes as needed (see Notes).

4. Click OK or press ↵ when done.

To Delete a Figure Box

1. Click on the figure. (If the figure is superimposed over text, first select Wrap Text Around Box in the Box Position and Size dialog box to remove the text overlay. See Notes.)

2. Press Delete.

To Size and Position a Box

Once selected, a figure box can be moved, enlarged, or reduced using the mouse or menu selections. With the mouse:

1. Click on the graphic box to display the box's positioning and sizing handles.

2. Click anywhere in the box and drag to move the box.

3. Click on any handle and drag to size the box.

4. Click the mouse in the document to deselect the image.

To size and position the box more precisely:

1. Choose Graphics ➤ Figure ➤ Position.

2. Enter a figure number and click OK. Then, select the desired options from Box Size and Position dialog box:

Box Type	Changes selected box to another type: Figure, Table Box, Text Box, User Box, or Equation
Anchor to	Anchors figure to selected Paragraph, Page, or Character and sets the Number of Pages to Skip (see Notes)

Vertical Position	Places the figure as Full Page, at the Top, Center or Bottom of the page, or prompts to Set Position in inches from the top of the page (the actual position depends on anchor type)
Horizontal Position	Places the figure at the Margin, Left; Margin, Right; Margin, Center; or Margin, Full (or at the Left, Right, Center, or Full width of a column); or prompts to Set Position in inches from the left margin (the actual position depends on anchor type)
Size	Sets a precise size for the box: Auto Both to restore original dimensions; Auto Width to enter a new height; Auto Height to enter a new width; and Set Both to enter your own measurements
Wrap Text Around Box	When selected, text does not overlay the box; when deselected, the text is superimposed on the graphics.

3. Click OK.

You can also rotate the image within the box using the mouse:

1. Double-click the graphic to be rotated.

2. Choose Edit ➤ Rotate or click the Rotate button.

3. Click the vertical axis to rotate the image 90 degrees counterclockwise.

4. Click the left axis to turn the image upside down.

5. Click and drag the right axis to rotate the image to any desired angle.

6. Click the Close button.

To Change the Appearance of the Box

Use the Box Options dialog box to set the borders, shading, distance from text, and captioning style number and position of any graphics box.

1.   Position the insertion point on or before the Figure Box code. Turn Reveal Codes on to see the codes.

2.   Choose Graphics ➤ *box type* ➤ Options.

3.   Select options from the resulting dialog box. The dialog boxes for each of the box types contain the same options.

Border Styles	Choose from **None**, **Single**, **Double**, **Dashed**, **Dotted**, **Thick**, or **Extra Thick** for the **Left**, **Right**, **Top**, or **Bottom** borders
Border Spacing	Enter the space from the box contents for the outside and inside **Left**, **Right**, **Top**, and **Bottom** borders
Gray Shading	Enter percent of shading, from 0 to 100, for the box interior
Minimum Offset from Paragraph	Specify the minimum distance from the top of the anchoring paragraph that a box can move before it is placed on the next page
Caption Numbering	Choose **Off**, **Numbers**, **Letters**, or **Roman** Numerals for the **First** and **Second** levels of captions numbers; you can also choose the **Style** pop-up menu to print numbers **Bold**, **Italic**, **Underlined**, or in **Small Caps**

Caption   Choose **B**elow, Outside; **A**bove,
Positioning   **O**utside; Below, **I**nside; or
                   Above, Inside to indicate the
                   relative position of captions to
                   the graphic box

4. Click OK or press ↵ when done.

To Create or Edit a Caption

Use the Caption Editor to write the caption text. Then use the Figure Options dialog box to select the caption style, position, and numbering scheme. You can use either the mouse or the menu system to select a caption for editing.

To use the mouse:

1. Position the mouse pointer on the graphics box.

2. Click the *right* mouse button.

3. Choose Edit **C**aption from the pop-up menu.

4. You'll see the word *Figure* and the figure number (assigned automatically). Type a caption or edit any of the existing text in the usual manner.

5. Choose **C**lose to return to your document.

To use the menu system:

1. Choose **G**raphics ➤ *box type* ➤ **C**aption.

2. Enter the number of the graphics box.

3. Choose OK.

4. You'll see the word *Figure* and the figure number (assigned automatically). Type a caption or edit any existing text in the usual manner.

5. Choose **C**lose to return to your document.

● **NOTES**   Each type of graphics box is numbered inde-
pendently, and each type of box initially has its own border style (see
Figure 8). You can retrieve figure files from a graphics file into Table

A figure box is framed with a single-line border.

A table box has thick top and bottom borders.

A text box has thick top and bottom borders and is shaded.

A user box has no border.

Figure 8: Some sample graphics with standard border options

or User boxes, but not into any of the other box types. When you select Create after choosing a User or Table box type, a dialog box appears, allowing you to choose an editor. Choose the editor for the type of material to be inserted; for example, to insert a graphic image into a Table box, choose Graphics ➤ Table Box ➤ Create, and then select Figure Editor.

You can leave a box empty, or use the Figure, Text, or Equation editor to edit the contents of the box. WordPerfect comes with many sample graphics images (.WPG files); you can also create your own or buy additional images.

Using the Figure Editor   The Figure Editor offers four groups of submenus: File, Edit, View, and Help. (See the Equations command reference for details of the Equation Editor and the Text Boxes command reference for the Text Editor options.)

The File menu selection provides four options in addition to Cancel and Close:

- Retrieve: Allows you to select a graphics file and open it in a figure box.

- Save As: If the graphics file was in another format (and WordPerfect had to convert it temporarily for its own use), this option allows you to save it as a .WPG file. The original file on disk remains unchanged.

- Graphic on Disk: By default, when you work with the Figure Editor, WordPerfect saves the graphic file as part of the document. This option lets you save it separately, potentially in a format other than .WPG. Saving graphics separately also conserves space in a document file.

- Box Position: This selection accesses the Box Position and Size dialog box.

The Edit menu selection provides the options listed below:

Move	Moves the figure a specified amount within the box

Rotate	Rotates figure within the box: Click vertical axis to rotate image 90 degrees counterclockwise; Click left axis to turn image upside down; Click right axis to rotate image to any desired angle
Scale	Enlarges or reduces the graphic or a portion of the graphic.
Mirror	Reverses the figure on its vertical axis
Invert	Changes displayed/printed image to complementary colors (black and white are left unchanged)
Outline	Displays the figure as line drawing
Black and White	Changes all colors in the figure to black
Edit All	Enables all editing options
Reset All	Resets all features to their original settings

The View menu selection turns the Button Bar on and off and allows you to change the setup of the Button Bar.

For more information on the Box Position and size dialog box, see "To Change the Appearance of the Box" above.

Anchor Types and Box Positioning   A box can be anchored to a specific paragraph, page, or character. You can set the anchor type through the Box Position and Size dialog box. Figure 9 illustrates the effects of various positioning and anchoring options.

- **Paragraph**: the box moves with the text that wraps around it. The graphics box code (e.g., [Fig Box]) must be at the beginning of the paragraph. If Auto Code Placement is on, WordPerfect automatically puts the code there.

- **Page**: The box remains at a fixed position on the page. To make sure that any changes in preceding text don't affect this position, begin with the insertion point at the beginning of the document. Create the box and choose Page as the anchor type in the Box Position and Size dialog box.

Examples of Anchoring Boxes

CHECK BOX

We start with a small graphic image that is anchored to this paragraph (the box's hidden code is just before the first character of this paragraph).

The box is sized small, and the text of the paragraph wraps around it.

DIPLOMA

Another case for anchoring a figure to a paragraph is when you want a figure to closely follow its callout in text.

For example, Figure 1 shows a diploma. To keep that figure near, but below, it's anchored to the top of the next paragraph. Its Horizontal Position is Full (the width of the column).

Figure 1.

Because the box is as wide as this column, no text wraps around the side of it.

TEXT BOX

The text box in the center of the page is anchored to the page. Its hidden code is at the top of the page. All text wraps around it. Page anchoring is the only way to create boxes that cross columns.

TABLE BOX

The Table box in the lower right corner of the page is

WordPerfect has lots of tools for aligning graphic boxes in columns

also anchored to the page (bottom right corner). Page anchoring was required here because we needed the table to be wider than one column.

FOOTER

The pencil symbol at the lower left corner of the page is actually in a footer. It's character-anchored, because that's the

only anchor type allowed in headers and footers.

IN-LINE GRAPHIC

Next we have a small graphic airplane in the text. The airplane graphic is in a character anchored User Box, and is sized small enough to fit on a line of text.

Small character-anchored graphics like that can be used as icons in text, margins, or in margin notes -- or perhaps for amusing pictures in children's books.

COLUMNS & LINES

The columns in this example are newspaper columns with a distance of .4" between them. Chapter 20 discusses multi-column layouts in detail.

The lines are all graphic lines with the Graphics ▸ Line menu options (see Chapter 5).

The table below shows the Column (horizontal) and Vertical position, as the length, of each vertical line.

Line	1st	2nd	3rd	4th
Column	1	2	1	2
Vertical	1.51	1.51	6.35	6.35
Length	2.83	2.83	3.45	2.08

Page 1

Figure 9: Graphics box positioning and anchoring options

- **Character**: the box is treated as an element of text in the line on which its code appears. The height of the box determines the height of the entire line.

When you set the vertical and horizontal positions for the box, the settings and actual location of the box depend on the anchor type as follows:

Vertical Position

Paragraph anchor: positions the box at an offset from the top of the paragraph. The default offset of 0" aligns the box with the top line of the paragraph; entering any other value moves the box down by the corresponding amount. For example, an offset of 0.5" aligns the top of the box half an inch below the top of the paragraph.

Page anchor: positions the box at the top, bottom, center, at a specific offset from the top of the page, or covering the full page.

Character anchor: aligns the box so that the top, bottom, or center of the box is even with the baseline of the line containing the graphics box code.

Horizontal Position

Paragraph anchor: aligns the box with the left or right margin, centers it between the two, or fills the space between the margins.

Page anchor: aligns the box with left or right margins or column edges, centers it between the margins of the full page or set columns, or fills the space between page or column margins. A Set Position measurement positions the box a set distance from the left edge of the page.

Character anchor: not allowed.

Renumbering Boxes   Graphics boxes are numbered consecutively by box type throughout the document. You can start with a new number within the document, such as, at the beginning of a major section. The maximum number for any box type is 2047, for first level numbers, and 31, for second level numbers. After reaching the maximum number, WordPerfect starts over from 1; for example, the next figure after Figure 3.31 is Figure 4.1.

To start renumbering boxes:

1. Position insertion point just before the box code (use Reveal Codes to make sure of position).

2. Choose **Graphics** ➤ box type ➤ **New Number**.

3. Enter the new figure number.

4. Click OK or press ↵.

See Also Advance, Border Styles, Codes, Equations, File Manager, Graphics Conversion, Initial Codes, Lists, Printer Select, Text Boxes

GRAPHICS CONVERSION

These procedures convert files created by various graphics programs into WordPerfect graphics files. WordPerfect graphics files can be inserted in your documents (see the Graphics command reference).

To Convert a Graphics File to WordPerfect Format

1. Choose **File** ➤ **Exit** (Alt+F4) to exit WordPerfect and access the Windows Program Manager. Or, click on the Word-Perfect Control-menu box (in the upper-left corner of the WordPerfect window) and choose **Switch To**, highlight the Program Manager and click the **Switch To** button.

2. Choose **File** ➤ **Run**.

3. By default, the GRAPHCNV.EXE program is installed in the **C:\WPC** directory. Type **\GRAPHCNV** and choose OK to start the program.

4. Enter the full path and name of the *input file*.

5. If necessary, edit path and name of the *output file*.

6. When prompted, press any key to exit the program.

● **NOTES** All graphics files must ultimately be converted to WordPerfect Graphics (WPG) format before WordPerfect can use them. If an image in a graphics box isn't already in WPG format, WordPerfect will convert it (the converted image is placed into a temporary file; the original graphic remains unchanged).

To speed up this process, use the GRAPHCNV program to convert a graphics file into WPG format (.WPG file name extension) and then specify the newly converted file name in graphics boxes.

GRAPHCNV can convert most popular graphics formats to WPG format.

You can use wildcards (* and ?) in the input file names. The conversion program will use the input filenames with the .WPG extension.

The GRAPHCNV options can also be typed on a single command line using various switches to activate special options for controlling color conversion, displaying conversion messages, controlling line widths, and so on.

For more information on GRAPHCNV, see the WordPerfect manual or choose File ➤ Run from the Windows Program Manager and enter **GRAPHCNV /h**.

See Also Graphics and Graphic Boxes

GRAPHICS LINES

You may place horizontal or vertical lines anywhere in your document with the Graphics Lines feature. You can set the line's thickness, length, and shading.

To Create a Line

1.   Position the insertion point to where you want the line (see Notes).

2.   Choose **Graphics ➤ Line ➤ Horizontal** (Ctrl+F11) or **Graphics ➤ Line ➤ Vertical** (Ctrl+Shift+F11).

3.   Specify the position and appearance of the line by using the various options (see Options below).

4.   Click OK until you return to the Edit screen.

To Edit a Line

You can edit a graphics line with the mouse or a menu. To edit a line with the mouse:

1.   Position the mouse pointer directly on the line. The insertion point will change to a four-headed arrow.

2.   Click the *right* mouse button.

3.   Choose Edit Horizontal (or Vertical) Line from the pop-up menu. It is the only available option.

4.   Edit the line by selecting the desired options from the Edit Horizontal (or Vertical) Line dialog box (see Options).

5.   Choose OK when done.

To access the Line Edit dialog box from the WordPerfect menu:

1.   Position the insertion point to the right of the line.

2.   Choose **Graphics ➤ Line ➤ Edit Horizontal** or **Graphics ➤ Line ➤ Edit Vertical**.

3.   Edit the line by selecting the desired options from the Edit Horizontal (or Vertical) Line dialog box (see Options).

4.   Choose OK when done.

To Move a Line Using the Mouse

You can reposition a line by dragging it to the new location with the mouse:

1. Position the tip of the mouse pointer directly on the line.

2. Click the left mouse button to select the line.

3. Drag the line to its new position.

4. Click elsewhere in the document window to deselect line.

To Delete a Line

You can delete a vertical or horizontal line by deleting its code.

1. Position the insertion point on the line code (turn on Reveal Codes, Alt+F3, to be sure of the position).

2. Press Delete.

Line Options   The dialog boxes for creating and editing both horizontal and vertical lines offer essentially the same options, some of which lead to pop-up menus that depend on the type of line selected:

Horizontal Position	Controls the horizontal positioning of the line. For *horizontal lines*, choose **L**eft, **R**ight, **C**enter, or **F**ull to align with respect to the margins, or choose **S**pecify and enter the measurement from the left edge of the page. For *vertical lines*, choose **L**eft or **R**ight to align with respect to the margins. Or choose **B**etween Columns and enter a column number to position the line between that column and the one to its right. Or choose **S**pecify and enter a measurement from the left edge of the page.

Vertical Position	Controls the vertical positioning of the line.
	For *horizontal lines*, choose **B**aseline to align the bottom of the line with the baseline of the text, or choose **S**pecify and enter a measurement from top of page.
	For *vertical lines*, choose **T**op, **B**ottom, Center, or **F**ull Page to align with respect to the margins, or choose **S**pecify and enter a measurement from the top of the page.
Length	Enter the line length in inches.
Thickness	Enter the desired thickness in inches. For *horizontal lines*, the line will expand downward if Vertical Position is set to Specify or expand upward if Vertical Position is set to Baseline. For *vertical lines*, the line will expand to the right, regardless of the Horizontal Position setting.
Gray Shading (% of black)	Enter the shading percentage to indicate the darkness of the line (100 = black).

See Also   Line Draw, Tables

HEADERS AND FOOTERS

You can print repeating text at the top (headers) or bottom (footers) of every page, odd pages only or even pages only.

To Create or Edit a Header or Footer

1.   Position the insertion point at the top of the page where the header/footer should take effect above any text.

2.   Choose Layout ➤ Page ➤ Headers (Alt+F9,H) or Layout ➤ Page ➤ Footers (Alt+F9,F).

3.   Choose Header/Footer **A** or Header/Footer **B**.

4.   Choose **Create** or **Edit**.

5.   Type or edit the header or footer (see Notes).

6.   Click **P**lacement to choose **E**very Page, **O**dd Pages, or **E**ven Pages. Then click **OK** to go to the Header (Footer) editing window.

7.   Choose **C**lose to return to the document window.

To Discontinue a Header or Footer

1.   Position the insertion point on or to the right of the appropriate [Header] or [Footer] code.

2.   Choose Layout ➤ Page ➤ Headers (Alt+F9,H) or Layout ➤ Page ➤ Footers (Alt+F9,F).

3.   Choose Header/Footer **A** or Header/Footer **B**.

4.   Choose **D**iscontinue.

● NOTES   You can define up to two headers (A and B) and two footers (A and B) to be used at any given time, and can change them as often as necessary. A header or footer will remain in effect until you define a different header or footer, suppress it (see the Page Suppress command reference), discontinue it, or delete it.

WordPerfect automatically adds an extra line after a header or before a footer.

Headers and footers may contain up to one page of text. The font of the header/footer is the same as that of the document, unless you change it in the Header/Footer editor.

Headers and footers display only when you print the document and on the Print Preview screen.

To delete a header or footer, choose **View** ➤ Reveal Codes (Alt+F3) and delete the appropriate [Header] or [Footer] code.

To suppress printing a header or footer, use the Suppress dialog box to specify those pages on which you don't want headers or footers (see the Page Suppress command reference).

Be sure to place the insertion point above any text on the page on which you want the header/footer to begin, if Auto Code Placement is off. Otherwise, the header/footer will not appear until the next page.

Using the Header/Footer Editor You can use all the usual editing features of WordPerfect, including graphics, fonts, the Speller, Date/Time Operations, and Thesaurus, while editing headers and footers.

To insert a page number into the header or footer, position the insertion point where you want the page number to appear. Then click on the Page Number button at the top of the Header/Footer edit page. The page number displays as ^B.

See Also Page Numbering, Page Suppress

HELP

WordPerfect provides both general help and context-sensitive help. General help provides information on basic WordPerfect tasks. Context-sensitive help information pertains to the task being performed or to a particular region of the screen. Help also lets you access information about Microsoft Windows.

To Access the Help Window

You can enter the Help feature by choosing Help from the menu bar, by clicking on the Help icon (if the Help window has been minimized), or by pressing F1. The results of pressing F1 depend on what was active when you pressed it:

- From a document window, the Help index is displayed.

- From the Help window, the Microsoft Windows Help topics are displayed.

- From menu items, dialog boxes, or special windows (such as the Speller), specific information pertaining to the item is displayed.

To Find Help Topics

To find information on a specific topic:

1. Choose Help from the menu bar.

2. Choose Index.

3. Scroll the list to find the desired topic.

4. Click on the name of the topic.

5. Choose File ➤ Exit or minimize the Help window (by clicking on the minimize ▼ button) when done. Minimizing the Help window makes subsequent access to Help faster.

To Save or Print Help Information

If you want to save a copy of the Help information in a document, you can use the Clipboard. While in the Help window:

1. Choose Edit ➤ Copy (Ctrl+Insert) to copy to the Clipboard.

2. Choose File ➤ Exit or minimize the Help window to return to the document window.

3. Choose Edit (from the document window menu) ➤ Paste (Shift+Insert).

To print a copy of the Help information, while in the Help window:

• Choose File ➤ Printer Setup (if necessary) ➤ Print Topic.

To Display Context-Sensitive Help

Two types of context-sensitive help are available: *Active* and *What Is*. Active help is accessed by choosing Help from an application menu or pressing F1. The help information that appears depends on what tasks you were doing when you asked for help. If you were in a dialog box, F1 displays help for the whole box or, if a specific option was selected, information for that option. If you were in a menu, Help displays information for the selected menu item.

With What Is help turned on, you get information by pointing and clicking the mouse on particular screen regions, menu items, buttons, or dialog box items. You can also press any key or key combination for explanatory information while in the What Is mode.

To enter the What Is help mode:

1. Choose **Help ➤ What Is**.

2. Point and click the mouse or press the desired key combination.

3. Choose File ➤ Exit when done, or minimize Help.

• **NOTES**   The Help window offers many options for accessing and viewing information about selected topics. The Help feature also presents a logical train of related items for you to browse through.

Help Menu Options   The initial Help menu gives you several options:

Index	Displays an alphabetic list of topics
Keyboard	Displays a list of topics relating to the CUA and WordPerfect keyboards and remapping information; it includes a list of shortcut keys

How Do I   Groups topics into types of tasks, such
                      as Basics, Edit, and Graphics

Glossary   Displays a list of words and phrases for
                      which there are pop-up definitions

Using Help   Displays information on using the
                      WordPerfect Help feature

What Is   Changes the keyboard and mouse to
                      the What Is mode. The mouse becomes
                      a question mark inside a bubble

About WordPerfect   Displays WordPerfect version and
                      copyright information

Once you have selected an option from the main Help menu, submenu and button options are offered. The submenu options are:

File   Open accesses any Help file.
              Print Topic prints selected information.
              Printer Setup selects and configures the printer.
              Exit (Alt+F4) closes the Help window.

Edit   Copy (Ctrl+Ins) copies any topic to the
              Clipboard.
              Annotate adds comments to a topic. A tiny
              paper clip appears next to the topic name,
              indicating that there are comments. Click on the
              paper clip to display the annotation.

Bookmark   Define marks a topic to which you want to
              return.
              The topic list enables you to return quickly to
              marked topics.

Help   Using Help (F1) displays information about
              using Microsoft Windows Help.
              About displays a message identifying the
              version of Microsoft Windows Help in use.

Button Bar Options   All Help windows display an array of button options for accessing Help topics:

Back   Moves to previous topics in the sequence you chose them.

Browse   Moves through a sequence of related topics. When you reach the first or last topic in the sequence, the button dims.

Index   Lists all the Help topics in alphabetical order.

Search   Displays a dialog box for you to select or enter keywords or phrases to search the Help topics.

Jump Terms and Pop-Up Definitions   Certain words and phrases, called *Jump Terms,* can lead you to related words or topics. These terms are underscored with a solid line. Click on the Jump Term to reach the new term.

Other words and phrases are underscored with dotted lines, indicating an underlying Pop-Up Definition. To view this definition, click on the word and hold the mouse button while you read the definition.

HYPHENATION

This feature keeps the right margin more evenly aligned by automatically hyphenating words when necessary. Various options enable you to choose a hyphenation dictionary, prompt for user assistance in hyphenating, set the hyphenation zone, and choose a hyphenation character.

To Turn Hyphenation On and Off

1. Choose Layout ➤ Line ➤ Hyphenation (Shift+F9,E).

2. Click the Hyphenation On check box in the Line Hyphenation dialog box to turn hyphenation on or off.

3. Click OK.

To Set the Hyphenation Zone

1. Position the insertion point in the paragraph where you want to change the hyphenation zone.

2. Choose Layout ➤ Line ➤ Hyphenation (Shift+F9,E).

3. Enter the percentage of line length to use for the left and right hyphenation zone boundaries.

4. Click OK.

The hyphenation zone is the portion of a line within which words will be hyphenated. The percentages set for its boundaries control where words must fall in order to be hyphenated. With hyphenation on, WordPerfect hyphenates words that start before the left boundary and extend past the right boundary. Set a wide zone to hyphenate fewer words, or a narrow zone to hyphenate more words.

To Set the Hyphenation Method

1. Choose File ➤ Preferences ➤ Environment.

2. Choose External or Internal.

3. Click OK.

The External method uses the large external dictionary contained in the file WP{WP}US.LEX (see the Location of Files command reference). You can add words to or delete words from this dictionary with the Hyphenation utility program. Run the WordPerfect Hyphenation Utility from DOS by typing **hyphen** at the DOS prompt. You can also use the utility program to create or change an exception dictionary, examine hyphen positions, look up words, and optimize the exception dictionary. And you can add or delete words with the Speller utility, which also uses the WP{WP}US.LEX dictionary.

The Internal method uses a smaller, internal dictionary built into WordPerfect. It doesn't offer the flexibility and utility of the larger dictionary, and it prompts you more often during automatic hyphenation. But, if you don't want to store the large external dictionary files on your hard disk, you can choose this option.

To Control the Hyphenation Prompt

1. Choose File ➤ Preferences ➤ Environment.

2. Indicate how WordPerfect should prompt the user when it can't find a word in the hyphenation dictionary:

- Never wraps the entire word to the next line if its hyphenation is not found.

- When Required prompts only if a word's hyphenation is not found.

- Always prompts whenever a word needs hyphenation.

3. Click OK.

● **NOTES**   When hyphenation is off, WordPerfect *wraps* (moves) a word to the next line when the word extends beyond the right margin. When hyphenation is on, WordPerfect will hyphenate words as you type or scroll through existing text.

For the most part, you'll just turn hyphenation on or off and use default settings for other hyphenation options (see below).

Responding to Hyphenation Prompts   If hyphenation is on and you have asked WordPerfect to prompt When Required or Always, the program will display the word in the Position Hyphen dialog box. Position the hyphen in the word by clicking between the first two letters and the letter that falls in the right hyphenation zone. Or, use the ← and → keys to position the hyphen, then click Insert Hyphen. See the Environment command reference for information on controlling whether the computer beeps when displaying the prompt.

Inserting Hyphenation Characters   You can also control hyphenation by manually inserting the special hyphenation

codes. Select Layout ➤ Line ➤ Special Codes (Shift+F9,O), and select
the appropriate hyphenation character from the Hyphenation Codes
section of the Insert Special Codes dialog box. The functions of the
various codes are:

Hyphen [–]

Used for words that include
normal hyphenation, such as
father-in-law. This hyphen
displays and prints as a dash (–).

Dash Character

Used to insert a hyphen in words
that should not be broken at the
end of a line, such as *tip-top*. You
can also insert a dash by pressing
Ctrl+–.

Soft Hyphen –

Used to hyphenate a word, if
hyphenation is necessary. Soft
hyphens are also inserted when
WordPerfect automatically
hyphenates a word or prompts
you to do so. This hyphen
displays and prints as a dash (–),
but only if hyphenation is
needed. You can also insert a soft
hyphen by pressing Ctrl+Shift+–.

Hyphenation soft return
[HyphSRt]

Used to *break* a word when
hyphenation is needed. It acts
like a soft hyphen, but simply
breaks the word; no dash
displays or prints.

Hyphenation Ignore **W**ord
[Hyph Ign Wrd]

Used at the beginning of a word
or after a soft hyphen to prevent
the hyphenation of the word. It
does not display or print.

See Also   Environment, Insert, Justification, Location of Files

INDENT

WordPerfect provides several ways to indent paragraphs or blocks of text, including left indent, double indent, and hanging indents. It also allows temporary margin release to realign text.

Indent temporarily indents the left margin of a paragraph. *Double Indent* temporarily indents the left and right margins of a paragraph by an equal amount. *Hanging Indent* keeps the first line in a paragraph flush with the left margin while indenting the remaining lines. A *margin release* moves the insertion point to the left one tab stop; if the insertion point is at the beginning of an indented line, that line returns to the left margin.

To indent the first line of a paragraph, simply press Tab.

To Left Indent a Paragraph

1. Place the insertion point where the indent should start (usually at the beginning of the paragraph).

2. Choose Layout ➤ Paragraph ➤ Indent (F7).

To Double Indent a Paragraph

1. Position the insertion point where the indent should start.

2. Choose Layout ➤ Paragraph ➤ Double Indent (Ctrl+Shift+F7).

To Insert a Hanging Indent

1. Position the insertion point at the beginning of the paragraph.

2. Choose Layout ➤ Paragraph ➤ Hanging Indent (Ctrl+F7).

To Release the Left Margin

1. Position the insertion point.

2. Choose Layout ➤ Paragraph ➤ Margin Release
(Shift+Tab).

● **NOTES** Indentation is based on the current tab settings. Each
time you issue an indent command, the paragraph's indentation will
move to the next tab stop.

When typing new text, indentation remains in effect until you press
Enter (↲) or choose Layout ➤ Page ➤ Page Break (Ctrl+↲).

See Also Lists, Margins, Tabs

INDEX

You can create a complete index for your document by using
WordPerfect's indexing features to a create concordance file or
mark index entries, define index location and numbering style, and
generate the index.

To Create a Concordance File

A concordance file contains all the words and phrases that you
want included in the index. You create this list and WordPerfect
searches through your document for every occurrence of the entry
and inserts appropriate page numbers in the index (see Notes).

To create a concordance file:

1. Choose File ➤ New (Shift+F4) to open a blank document
window.

2. Type the list of words and expressions to be included in
the index. Place each on a separate line.

3. Choose File ➤ Save (Shift+F3) and enter a file name in the
Save As text box. Then choose Save or press ↲.

4. Sort the list alphabetically by using Tools ➤ Sort to speed index generation and save it.

When you define the index, you will enter the name of the concordance file.

To Mark Index Entries within a Document

You may mark each index entry as a heading in itself, as a subheading under another heading, or as both a heading and a subheading.

1. Position the insertion point anywhere in a word you want to index, or select a phrase to index.

2. Choose Tools ➤ Mark Text ➤ Index (F12,I).

3. The text you marked appears in the Heading text box. Click OK if you want it to be a heading only.

4. If you want the marked text to be a subheading instead, type the word or phrase you want to use as the heading (for example, if "German Shepherd" is your subheading, "Dogs" might be the main heading), and then select the Subheading text box. The marked text will appear there.

5. Choose OK.

To Define the Index
Location and Page Numbering Style

1. Move the insertion point to the end of the document.

2. Optionally, choose Layout ➤ Page ➤ Page Break or press Ctrl+↵ to create a page break.

3. Optionally, enter a title for the index.

4. Choose Tools ➤ Define ➤ Index (Shift+F12,I).

5. Enter the concordance file name, or press ↵ if you aren't using a concordance file (see Notes).

6.   Choose a numbering style:

No Numbering	Includes entries, but no page numbers
Text #	Page numbers are preceded by a space
Text [#]	Page numbers are in parentheses
Text #	Page numbers are flush right
Text.......#	Dot leaders precede flush right page numbers

7.   Choose OK.

To Generate an Index

When all entries have been marked and the location and numbering style have been defined, you are ready to generate the index.

- Choose Tools ➤ Generate ➤ Yes (Alt+F12,Y).

● **NOTES**   You can create multiple index headings or subheadings for the same word or phrase by marking entries more than once. The word or phrase being indexed need not match its heading or subheading. For example, it's an indexing convention that gerunds should not be used as headings. In a book on wildlife observation, the phrase "Identifying Tracks" might be a chapter title. The indexer would mark the phrase and then, in the Mark Index dialog box, edit the phrase to read "Tracks, Identifying."

To delete an index entry in the document, choose View ➤ Reveal Codes (Alt+F3) and delete the appropriate [Index:] code.

Concordance Files   You can place entries in a separate concordance file in addition to, or instead of, marking entries in a document or subdocument. The concordance file contains a list of words or phrases to be indexed. Press ↵ after typing each word or phrase.

WordPerfect will generate an index entry whenever a phrase in the document *exactly* matches a phrase in the concordance file. Uppercase and lowercase entries (e.g., "TREES" and "trees") are treated the same.

Concordance file entries are automatically used as index headings. For more control over the headings and subheadings, you can mark concordance file entries as outlined under "To Mark Index Entries within a Document" above.

For quicker indexing, sort the concordance file alphabetically.

See Also   Generate, Master Document, Page Numbering, Selecting Text, Sorting and Selecting

INITIAL CODES

Initial codes let you predefine a format for all new documents or for the current document only. They can be examined and edited from anywhere in the document.

To Change Initial Codes for All New Documents

1. Choose File ➤ Preferences ➤ Initial Codes.

2. Choose the formatting features as you would when setting them for an individual document.

3. Choose Close when done.

To Change Initial Codes for the Current Document Only

1. Choose Layout ➤ Document ➤ Initial Codes (Ctrl+Shift+F9,C).

2. Choose the formatting features in the usual manner.

3. Choose Close.

To Choose an Initial Font for a Document

1.   Choose Layout ➤ Document ➤ Initial Font
(Ctrl+Shift+F9,F).

2.   Choose the font.

3.   Enter the point size (scalable fonts only).

4.   Choose OK.

● **NOTES**   You can define initial codes for these features: Column Definition and Column On; Decimal/Align Character; Font; Footnote and Endnote Number and Options; Graphics Box Number and Options; Hyphenation On/Off; Hyphenation Zone; Justification; Kerning; Language; Line Height, Numbering, and Spacing; Margins; New Page Number, Style, and Position; Paper Size; Suppress Page Format; Tab Settings; Text Color; Underline Spaces and Tabs; Widow/Orphan On/Off; and Word and Letter Spacing. Other codes and text have no effect.

Initial codes do not display in the Reveal Codes screen but they do affect the entire document, including its headers and footers.

Changing initial codes for all documents only affects new documents, not existing ones.

Initial codes for the current document override initial codes for all documents. Formatting codes entered into the document itself override all initial codes settings.

Define initial codes in the primary file when performing a merge operation so that they will repeat every time you use the primary file.

Define the Paper Size in initial codes to avoid printing only one entry per page when creating mailing labels.

You can edit initial codes from anywhere in the document by selecting Layout ➤ Document ➤ Initial Codes; you do not have to go to the top of the document.

See Also   Codes, Fonts, Merge Operations, Paper Size, and index entries for features listed above.

INSERT

In Insert mode, new text, blank lines, and most codes you type are inserted into existing text at the insertion point. Alternatively, Typeover mode replaces existing text. Press the Insert key to switch between modes.

● **NOTES**   WordPerfect is normally in Insert mode. **To insert new text or unpaired codes**, move the insertion point to where the new text or codes should begin, then type the text or insert the codes using pull-down menus or keyboard shortcuts.

To insert blank lines into existing text, move the insertion point to the left edge of the line that should appear below the blank lines. Press ↵ once for each line you want to insert.

To insert a blank line as you type, press ↵ twice at the end of the line. (Continue pressing ↵ to add additional blank lines.)

To insert paired formatting codes as you type, choose the pull-down menu option for the paired code or press its shortcut key, and then type the text. Press →, or choose the menu option, or press the shortcut key again to move beyond the paired codes.

To insert paired formatting codes into existing text, select the text, and then choose the pull-down menu option or press the paired code shortcut key.

Inserting Special Formatting Characters   Special formatting codes, including Hard Tab codes with or without dot leaders, Hyphenation codes, hard space codes, End Centering/ Alignment codes, Decimal Align Characters, and Thousands Separators, can be inserted into your document through the Layout menu:

1. Choose Layout ➤ Line ➤ Special Codes (Shift+F9, O).
2. Select the desired codes from the Insert Special Codes dialog box.
3. Choose Insert when done.

See Also   Document Window, Font Attributes, Insertion Point, Macros, Selecting Text, Special Characters, Typeover

INSERTION POINT

The insertion point is usually a small, blinking vertical bar that indicates where the next character that you type will appear in the document window. On the Reveal Codes window, the insertion point is a solid block, usually with a colored background.

To Move the Insertion Point with the Mouse

The mouse pointer is usually a moving I beam on the screen. This pointer can be used to move the insertion point to different parts of the document.

- To move to any character that is *visible* on the screen, position the I beam (mouse pointer) just before the character and click the left mouse button.

- To scroll to parts of the document that are *not visible* on the screen, click on the desired scroll bar arrow or drag the scroll box in the direction of the characters you want to see. Release the mouse button to stop scrolling. Then click to position the insertion point on the screen.

To Move the Insertion Point with the Keyboard

Many keys and key combinations (e.g., arrow keys, Home, End) move the insertion point to different places in your document. You may find some of these options easier and more precise than scrolling with the mouse. For most operations, you can move the insertion point by pressing the keys shown in Table 9.

● **NOTES**   You must position the insertion point before adding, changing, deleting, or moving text and most formatting codes. You can either type over or insert characters at the insertion point.

Table 9: Keyboard methods for moving the insertion point (most operations)

To Move To	Press
Beginning of document (after any codes)	Ctrl+Home
Beginning of document (before any codes)	Ctrl+Home,Ctrl+Home
Beginning of line (after any codes)	Home
Bottom of screen (then down one screen at a time)	PgDn
Down one line	↓
Down one paragraph	Ctrl+↓
End of document (after any codes)	Ctrl+End
End of line (after any codes)	End
Far left end of line (before any codes)	Home,Home
First line on previous page	Alt+PgUp
First line on next page	Alt+PgDn
Left one character	←
Left one word	Ctrl+←
Right one character	→
Right one word	Ctrl+→
Top of screen (then up one screen at a time)	PgUp
Up one line	↑
Up one paragraph	Ctrl+↑

You can not move the insertion point past the last or before the first character or code in a document.

If the insertion point does not seem to move when you are at the document window, it is probably resting on a hidden code. Continue moving the insertion point past the code, or turn on Reveal Codes (choose **View** ➤ Reveal **C**odes or press Alt+F3) to make the code visible.

See Also   Codes, Document Window, Go To, Mouse

JUSTIFICATION

Justification aligns text along the left or right margins, or both, or centers it on the page. You can set the justification for a single line, selected text, or the entire document.

To Justify Text

The quickest way to begin justification is to choose the desired placement from the ruler:

1. Choose **View** ➤ **R**uler (Alt+Shift+F3) to display the ruler.

2. Position the insertion point in the paragraph where you want justification to begin, or select a portion of existing text to be justified.

3. Click and hold the Justification button.

4. Choose desired justification from the drop-down menu.

    Left justification aligns text against the left margin, leaving the right margin ragged (uneven).

    Right justification aligns text against the right margin, leaving the left margin ragged.

    Center justification centers text between margins, and is similar to centering each line.

Full justification aligns text evenly against both the left and right margins. WordPerfect expands or compresses spaces between words to even out the line, according to the Word Spacing Justification Limits. (See the Typesetting command reference.)

An alternative method is to use the menu system:

1. Position the insertion point as above.

2. Choose Layout ➤ Justification.

3. Choose Left, **Right,** Center, or Full.

To Justify a Single Line

1. Select the text or prepare to enter a new line.

2. Choose Layout ➤ Line ➤ (Shift+F9).

3. Choose Center (Shift+F7) or Flush Right (Alt+F7).

● **NOTES**   Justification takes effect from the beginning of the paragraph in which the insertion point is located if Auto Code Placement is set on. If not, justification begins at the insertion point position. Justification continues to the end of the document or until changed again.

Line justification affects only a single line or selected text without continuing to the rest of the document.

Document justification is ignored by tables. The position of the table on the page is determined by the Position option in the Table Options dialog box.

See Also   Auto Code Placement, Center, Flush Right, Hyphenation, Initial Codes, Selecting Text, Tables, Typesetting

KEYBOARD LAYOUT

You can choose a predefined keyboard layout, create and edit your own custom keyboard layout, and assign keystrokes to macros and text strings. WordPerfect for Windows supplies two keyboard layouts: the default Common User Access (CUA) layout, which has the same function key assignments as other Windows applications; and the WordPerfect 5.1 layout, with the same key assignments as DOS versions of WordPerfect. Both layouts are illustrated in the inside covers of this book.

To Change a Keyboard Layout

1. Choose File ➤ Preferences ➤ Keyboard.

2. Choose Select from the Keyboard dialog box.

3. Highlight the desired keyboard file in the Select Keyboard File dialog box and choose Select.

4. Choose OK.

To return to the default keyboard layout, choose Default (CUA) from the Keyboard dialog box and choose OK.

To Create and Edit a Custom Keyboard Layout

You can create your own custom keyboard layout to assign frequently performed operations, text, or macros to a single keystroke or a combination of keystrokes. Invoke the Keyboard Editor, make your assignments, and save the changes in a named file with the .WWK extension.

1. Choose File ➤ Preferences ➤ Keyboard.

2. Choose Create or Edit, and press a key or a key combination.

3. In the Assignable Items box, you can use the Item Types pop-up menu to select the type of item displayed in the accompanying list:

- Commands: WordPerfect commands (the default)

- Menus: WordPerfect pull-down menus and sub-menus

- Text: user-created, unformatted text (up to 4000 characters)

- Macros: user-defined processes

- User-defined macros and text must be added to their respective lists before a keystroke can be assigned to them.

4. Select an item to use as the new assignment for the keystroke.

5. Click Assign.

6. Repeat steps 3–5 to make more changes, as needed.

7. Choose Save As, and edit the path and file name as needed.

8. Choose Save. If the file exists, you'll be asked whether to replace the previous version.

● **NOTES**   You can choose from several predefined keyboards, or set up your own special keyboards with shortcut keys for operations you perform frequently.

Keyboard definitions (.WWK files) and macro files (.WCM) are stored in the directory specified in Location of Files.

The Keyboard Editor dialog box displays the current keystrokes you have entered and wish to assign to an item. You also have the option of having the keystrokes displayed as shortcut keys in the appropriate menu.

An additional remapping is available to change the Home key to function as it does in DOS WordPerfect 5.1.

See Also   Environment, Location of Files, Macros

LANGUAGE

WordPerfect enables you to switch to different languages for various language-dependent features, such as date display, hyphenation, sorting, and spell checking. You can apply these rules to those parts of your document that are in a foreign language.

To Choose a Different Language

Before you begin typing foreign text:

1. Position the insertion point to where the new language will take effect.
2. Choose Tools ➤ Language.
3. Select the language from the displayed Current Language List. Or, select Other from the list and enter a two-letter language code in the text box.
4. Click OK.

To Avoid Spell Checking a Section of Your Document

If sections in your document contain many scientific or technical terms that are not in the Speller, you can save time by skipping the spell check for that section. To do so, you can create a false language code for which WordPerfect has no speller.

1. Position insertion point at beginning of the section.
2. Choose Tools ➤ Language.
3. Select Other from the Current Language list, choose the Other text box, and type **XX**.
4. Choose OK.

Be sure to revert to the original language at the end of the section. Then, when the document is finished and you run the Speller, WordPerfect will indicate that it has no spell checker for language

XX. Choose **S**kip Language to continue spell checking the remainder of the document.

● **NOTES**   The currently selected language determines which Speller, Thesaurus, and Hyphenation files WordPerfect will use; the sort order for Sort features; and the language used to display date text and "(continued...)" messages in footnotes (if entered in document Initial Codes).

You can control text for certain features (such as month names) in various languages by editing the WP.LRS language resource file.

See Also   Initial Codes

LINE DRAW

This command offers you a way to draw lines in your document using the arrow keys. It also enables you to draw lines made up of characters in the WordPerfect Character Set. Line Draw does not, however, allow you to vary the gray shading or line thickness. You must use the Graphics Line command to do that.

To Draw Lines

1.   Move the insertion point to the location where the line will begin.

2.   Choose Tools ➤ Line Draw (Ctrl+D). The document window switches to Draft Mode, and the Line Draw dialog box is displayed.

3.   Select a preset character, or use a WordPerfect character (see Notes), to be used in composing the line.

4.   Use the arrow keys (←, →, ↑, ↓) to draw the line.

5.   Choose Close.

To Erase a Line

You erase a line in nearly the same manner as you drew it:

1.   Select **T**ools ➤ Line Draw (Ctrl+D).

2.   Select **E**rase in the Mode area of the Line Draw dialog box.

3.   Use the arrow keys to move the cursor back over the line. The line segments the cursor passes over will disappear.

4.   Choose Close.

● **NOTES**   You cannot use the mouse to move the insertion point while you are in the Line Draw dialog box. You can, however, select the Move option in the dialog box and then move the insertion point with the arrow keys.

Quick Draw Keystrokes   To speed line drawing, four Quick Draw keystrokes are available:

Home or Ctrl+←	Extends the line to left margin
End or Ctrl+→	Extends the line to right margin
Ctrl+↑	Extends the line to top margin
Ctrl+↓	Extends the line to bottom margin

Changing Line Characters   If you do not want to draw a line with one of the 11 preset characters, you can select any of the other special WordPerfect characters:

1.   Choose **C**haracter in the Line Draw dialog box.

2.   Type a character into the Line Draw Character dialog box.

3.   Choose OK.

Or…

1.   Choose **C**haracter in the Line Draw dialog box.

2.   Press Ctrl+W to display the WordPerfect Characters dialog box.

3.   Select the desired character from the default ASCII character set, or click on the Set button to choose from a pop-up list of other character sets.

4. Choose Insert.

5. Choose Close and then OK.

See Also Graphics and Graphic Boxes, Repeat, Special Characters, Tables, Typeover

LINE HEIGHT

Line height is the distance between the baseline of one line and the baseline of the next. You can set the fixed line height to the default value or specify a different height. You can also specify the amount of white space that appears between lines and between paragraphs.

To Set Line Height

1. Move the insertion point to the position where the new line height is to take effect.

2. Choose Layout ➤ Line ➤ Height (Shift+F9,H).

3. Select either **A**uto or Fixed.

4. If you selected Fixed, enter a line height measurement in inches or points, depending on the units of measure you have specified (see the Units of Measure command reference).

5. Choose OK.

To Set the Space between Lines and Paragraphs

You can specify the amount of space that shows between lines, between paragraphs, or both. These measurements need not be the same.

1. Move the insertion point to the place where the new height adjustment is to take effect.

2. Choose Layout ➤ Typsetting.

3. Enter a height in the Between Lines [SRt] text box and/or the Between Paragraphs [HRt] text box (see Notes).

4. Choose OK.

• NOTES If you choose Auto (the default), WordPerfect adds 2 points of space to proportionally spaced fonts and automatically adjusts line height to match the space required for the largest font on a line.

If you choose Fixed, lines will have the height you specify and be evenly spaced, regardless of the font size. Fixed line heights are often used with baseline placement for typesetting (see the Typesetting command reference).

Setting the line height has no effect on printers that can only print 6 lines per inch.

Positive line height adjustment amounts increase the line height and negative amounts decrease the height. The amounts are usually in inches unless you have changed the Units of Measure.

See Also Auto Code Placement, Font, Initial Codes, Typesetting, Units of Measure

LINE NUMBERING

You can print line numbers on a document. They do not appear in the document window but can be viewed with Print Preview. You can change the numbering scheme and position of the number on the line.

To Set Line Numbering

1. Position the insertion point to where you want line numbering to begin.

2.   Choose **Layout ➤ Line ➤ Numbering** (Shift+F9,N).

3.   Specify the options you want for line numbers:

Off   Turns off line numbering

Restart Each Page   Starts line numbers with 1 at
                                   the beginning of a new page

Continuous   Numbers lines continuously
                                   through the document

Position from Left Edge   Enter a measurement from
                                   the left edge of the paper

Starting Number   Enter a starting line number
                                   (the default is 1)

Number Every   Numbers only every nth
                                   line; enter a number (e.g., **5**
                                   will number every fifth line)

Count Blank Lines   **M**ark the check box to count
                                   blank lines or leave it blank
                                   to prevent them from being
                                   numbered or counted

4.   Choose OK.

To discontinue line numbering, choose **Off** in step 3 above.

● **NOTES**   Footnotes and endnotes are always counted in line
numbers; headers and footers are not.

See Also   Auto Code Placement, Initial Codes, Print Preview

LINE SPACING

Line spacing determines the number of lines that will be inserted
for each Soft Return [SRt] and Hard Return [HRt] code. Single spacing is the default.

You can use either the ruler or the menu system to set the desired line spacing.

To Set Line Spacing

To use the ruler:

1. To display the ruler, select **View ➤ Ruler** (Alt+Shift+F3).

2. Move the insertion point to the location where the new setting should take effect or select the text.

3. Click and hold the line spacing button on the far right of the ruler.

4. Choose one of the three line spacing settings from the popup menu (1.0, 1.5, or 2.0).

The line spacing button always displays the current setting.

To use the menu system:

1. Move the insertion point to the location where the new line spacing should take effect, or select a block of text.

2. Choose **Layout ➤ Line ➤ Spacing** (Shift+F9,S).

3. Enter a whole number or fraction. The buttons beside the text box automatically increase or decrease the value in steps of half a line.

4. Choose OK.

Double-clicking the line spacing button in the ruler will display the Line Spacing dialog box as in step 3 above.

● **NOTES**   The value you set for line spacing is multiplied by the line height to determine the actual distance between lines (e.g., if line spacing is 2.5 and line height is 0.5", lines will be printed 1.25" apart, baseline to baseline).

See Also   Auto Code Placement, Initial Codes, Line Height, Typesetting

LINKING DATA

When you *link* data in a file created by another application to a WordPerfect document, the data will be inserted at the specified point and then updated automatically in the WordPerfect document whenever it changes in the source application.

WordPerfect for Windows offers two linking methods: the Windows Dynamic Data Exchange (DDE) Link, and the Spreadsheet Link (which is shared with DOS versions of WordPerfect). Besides working only with spreadsheet files, the latter method is compatible with fewer applications. With DDE Link, however, you must first open the other application and then open WordPerfect in order to update the data. Spreadsheet Link reads the data from disk and updates it each time you open the WordPerfect document.

DDE Link

Use this method to import any type of data from any application that supports DDE (that is, from any Windows application). You first create the link by inserting link codes in the WordPerfect destination file, identifying the source, and naming the link. WordPerfect can then update your file automatically when the data changes in the source file.

You can also copy data from another Windows application into the Clipboard and then "paste link" it into your WordPerfect document. This operation is similar to an ordinary paste from the Clipboard, except that you establish a link for updating. All DDE Link operations are accessed through the Edit ➤ Link dialog box.

To Create or Edit a DDE Link

1. Begin by first opening the source file and then the WordPerfect destination file.

2. Position the insertion point at the spot where the linked data is to appear.

3. Choose Edit ➤ Link ➤ Create.

4. Specify a Source File and Item name; the Destination File is the currently active document (see Notes).

5. Enter a Link Name.

6. Select the update mode (**Automatic** or **Manual**).

7. Select the Storage Type (**Text** or **Graphics**).

8. Choose OK.

9. Repeat the steps above until all links have been created in your document.

To Edit an Existing Link

1. Choose Edit ➤ Link ➤ Edit.

2. Select the link name from the displayed list.

3. Make necessary changes by typing a new name, selecting a new file from a list of open files, or selecting an update option.

4. Choose OK.

To Delete a Link from Your Document

1. Position the insertion point at the link code.

2. Choose Edit ➤ Link ➤ Delete.

3. Select the link name from the list box or leave the **All** Links check box selected. Click OK and select **Yes** when asked to confirm the deletion.

To Paste Link Data via the Clipboard

1. Open both files. In the source file, copy the data to the Clipboard.

2. In the WordPerfect document, place the insertion point where the linked data should appear.

3. Select Edit ➤ Link ➤ Paste Link.

● **NOTES** Both source and destination files must be open before automatic updating can take place and the source should be opened first. If you had already opened the WordPerfect file, choose Edit ➤ Link ➤ Update to notify WordPerfect that the source file is open and automatic updating can begin.

If you are linking an entire file (for example, a graphic image), no further identification is necessary; move on to the Link Name text box.

If you are linking only part of a file (for example, a database record field or a range of spreadsheet cells), enter the name you've given that item in the other application. Type a vertical bar (¦) to separate the item name from the file name.

If you copied the data from the other application into the Clipboard, its description will appear in the Source File and Item Name text box automatically.

If the source file was not already open, enter the application name, file name, and item (if any), separated by ¦ characters.

WordPerfect will use the name you assign under Link Name in the Create DDE Link dialog box to identify the link in subsequent DDE Link dialog boxes.

See Also Move, Spreadsheet Link

LISTS

You can create up to 10 lists of tables, figures, maps, illustrations, or anything else for each document. Each list can have any of the five available numbering styles. The three steps to creating lists are: marking the text for the list items, defining the list location and numbering style, and generating the list. You do not need to mark captions for any of the WordPerfect graphics boxes; WordPerfect maintains lists of these items automatically.

To Mark a List Item

1. Select the text, including any codes that should appear in the list.

2. Choose Tools ➤ Mark Text ➤ List (F12,L).

3. Select the list number (1–10).

4. Choose OK.

To Define the List Location and Page Numbering Style

1. Move the insertion point to the location where you want the list to appear, usually at the end of the document.

2. If desired, choose Layout ➤ Page ➤ Page Break (Ctrl+↵) to place the list on a separate page.

3. Optionally, enter a title for the list and press ↵ as desired to add blank lines.

4. Choose Tools ➤ Define ➤ List (Shift+F2,L).

5. Enter the number of the list you want to define (1–10).

6. Choose a Page Numbering Format for the list:

No Numbering	Includes list items, but no page numbers
Text #	Page numbers follow text, separated by a space
Text (#)	Page numbers are in parentheses following the text, separated by a space
Text #	Page numbers are flush right
Text.....#	Dot leaders precede flush-right page numbers

7. Choose OK.

Repeat the steps above for each list in the document.

To Generate a List

The last step is to generate the list. The list may be edited after generation, but your edits will be lost if the list is regenerated. Since the list normally includes page numbers, you should also regenerate the list whenever changes in the document affect pagination. To generate the list:

- Choose **T**ools ➤ **G**enerate ➤ **Y**es (Alt+F12,Y).

● **NOTES**   You can create lists for an individual document or for a master document. Place the list definition in the master document, *not* in a subdocument.

WordPerfect automatically marks the text of captions for figure, table, text, user-defined or equation boxes and assigns them to lists 6, 7, 8, 9, and 10, respectively. Any text you mark to be included in one of these lists will be treated as a list item.

Generated list items will be in the order in which they appear in the document.

To delete a list item, choose **V**iew ➤ **R**eveal Codes (Alt+F3) and delete the appropriate [Mark:List] or [End Def] code. Then regenerate the list.

You may want to add a New Page Numbering code at the top of the page containing the list or at the top of the first page after your list.

See Also   Equations, Generate, Graphics and Graphic Boxes, Index, Page Numbering, Selecting Text, Table of Authorities, Table of Contents

LOCATION OF FILES

The Location of Files command lets you indicate which directories will be in effect when you start WordPerfect. It tells WordPerfect where to find and store various types of files. You may save files to directories other than the default by typing in the full path name when you save the file.

To Set the Default Locations for Files

1. Choose File ➤ Preferences ➤ Location of Files.

2. Type a directory or path name in each text box (see Options).

3. Click OK.

Or...

1. Choose File ➤ Preferences ➤ Location of Files.

2. Press the list button (the small file folder icon) opposite the desired file category.

3. Select a directory from the displayed list.

4. Click OK.

● **NOTES** When you install WordPerfect, most file locations are pre-defined, but you can change these settings as necessary. Word-Perfect will automatically look in these locations whenever you enter a file name (such as BICYCLE.WPG) instead of a full pathname (such as C:\WPWIN\BICYCLE.WPG). To override the default location, supply a full path name.

WordPerfect will not move existing files from the old location to the new one.

All directories must exist before you can use them in location settings. If you specify one that does not exist, WordPerfect will ask if you want to create it.

• OPTIONS

Backup Files

Enter a directory for timed backup files WP{WP}.BK1 and WP{WP}.BK2. If this directory is blank, WordPerfect uses the directory where WPWIN.EXE is located.

Documents

Enter a directory for saved document files.

Graphic Files

Enter a directory for graphics files (.CGM, .WPG, .EPS, etc.).

Printer Files

Enter a directory for the WordPerfect printer files (.ALL and .PRS).

Spreadsheets

Enter a directory for the spreadsheets that you link to or import into your documents.

Macros/Keyboards/
Button Bars Files

Enter a directory for macro files, keyboard layout files and Button Bar Files.

Styles

Enter a directory for style files (.STY). Then enter a file name for your default library of style (such as C:\WPWIN\LIBRARY.STY).

Thesaurus/Speller/
Hyphenation

Enter a directory for the Main thesaurus (.THS), Speller (.LEX), and external hyphenation dictionary (.HYD). Then enter a directory for the Supplementary Speller (.SUP) files.

See Also   Backup, Graphics and Graphic Boxes, Hyphenation, Keyboard Layout, Macros, Printer Select, Save/Save As, Speller, Spreadsheets, Styles, Thesaurus

MACROS

Macros let you record the commands (that is, the results of the keystrokes and mouse selections) that perform a certain task and play them back just the way they were recorded. Macros can be assigned for playback to a menu, a button, or to a keystroke combination. Advanced features include a programming language for defining fully interactive macros and displaying message windows.

The topic of macro programming is beyond the scope of this book. This entry presents techniques for recording, playing back, and assigning macros.

Since WordPerfect for Windows macros differ greatly from Word-Perfect 5.1 macros, WordPerfect for Windows includes a utility for converting 5.1 macros to the new format. This conversion utility is discussed in the Macro Conversion entry.

To Record a Macro

1. Choose **Macro** ➤ **Record** (Ctrl+F10). You will see the Record Macro dialog box.

2. In the **Filename** text box, type the macro name (up to 8 characters).

3. Optionally, in the **Descriptive Name** text box, type a description of the macro.

4. In the Abstract text box, type a more detailed summary of the macro's operations, if desired.

5. Choose **Record**. The *Recording Macro* message appears in the status bar.

6. If the macro already exists, WordPerfect will ask if you want to replace it. If you choose Yes, recording will begin. If No, you will return to the Record Macro dialog box.

7. Type the keystrokes whose results you want to record or select menu items with the mouse (see Notes).

8. Choose Macro ➤ Stop (Ctrl+Shift+F10). The *Recording Macro* message disappears from the status bar.

To Play a Macro

Once the macro is recorded, you can play it back and all the keystrokes will be repeated just as you entered them. There are several ways to play a macro: choose it from a dialog box, select it from a menu, click a button, or press a keystroke combination.

To play a macro from the Play Macro dialog box:

1. Choose Macro ➤ Play (Alt+F10).

2. Select the macro from the displayed list, or type in the macro name. The list contains only files with the .WCM extension unless you change the file filter in the Filename text box.

3. Choose Play.

To play a macro from the Macro menu, choose Macro and select the macro name. (You must have assigned the macro to the menu.)

If you have assigned your macro to a button on the Button Bar, simply click that button to play the macro.

To play a macro assigned to a certain keystroke combination, simply press that combination.

To Assign a Macro to the Macro Menu

You can assign up to nine macros to the Macro drop-down menu. When you want to play the macro, open the Macro menu and click on the menu selection. To assign a recorded macro to the menu:

1. Choose Macro ➤ Assign to Menu.

2. Choose Insert from the Assign Macro to Menu dialog box.

3. You will see the Insert Macro Menu Item dialog box. To specify a Macro Name, you can either type a full path and file name or click on the accompanying button, select a macro from the Select File dialog box, and click Select.

4. Type a description of the macro (up to 30 characters) as you wish it to appear on the Macro menu.

5. Choose OK twice to return to the document window.

After the assignment, you may change or remove the menu item. To edit the menu text:

1. Choose **Macro ➤ Assign to Menu.

2. Select the macro menu item to be edited.

3. Choose **Edit**.

4. Make necessary changes to the macro name menu text.

5. Choose OK twice to return to the document window.

To remove a menu item from the menu, after selecting the desired macro in step 2 above, choose **Delete** followed by OK.

To Assign a Macro to a Button

When you assign a macro to a button, the button is displayed as a cassette tape icon with the name of the macro. To assign a macro to a button:

1. Choose **View ➤ Button Bar Setup ➤ Edit**.

2. Choose **Assign Macro to Button**.

3. Select the desired macro from the list (double-click on the macro name or highlight and choose **Assign**).

4. Choose OK.

To Assign a Macro to Keystrokes

You can assign macros to key combinations, beginning with one of the modifier keys.

1. Choose **File ➤ Preferences ➤ Keyboard ➤ Create**.

2. In the Keyboard Editor dialog box, click **Item** Types and select M**a**cros from the drop-down list.

3. Choose A**dd**.

4. Select the macro file from the Import Macro to Keyboard dialog box and click **Import**.

5. Enter the desired keystroke combination. If it is already assigned to a macro, the current assignment will appear in the Change Assignment box.

6. If the combination is acceptable, click Assign in the Keyboard Editor dialog box.

7. To save the assignment to a Keyboard file, click **S**ave As.

8. Select or enter a Keyboard file name and click **S**ave.

9. Click OK until you return to your document.

• **NOTES**   Macros are compiled prior to playback, with their source and object code stored at the beginning of the document.

The WordPerfect macro language provides hundreds of commands that allow you to write complex macros that incorporate mathematical and logical operations, and involve user interaction. See the WordPerfect Macros manual for more information.

Recording the Macro   Everything you type—mistakes and all—will be recorded. You can edit the macro or re-record it to correct mistakes. Macro files are ordinary document files and may be edited the same way as any document. All WordPerfect macros must contain the command **Application (wp.wpwp)** so that the Windows macro system recognizes the macro as a WordPerfect macro. WordPerfect enters this command automatically when you record a macro. Other commands can be found in the WordPerfect Macros manual.

You may specify an extension other than the default .WCM. However, only files with the .WCM extension are displayed in the list when you choose Play from the macro menu. To view the names of other macro files, change the file filter.

You can use the mouse to choose pull-down menu options, cycle through windows, or close files while recording a macro, but you *cannot* use it to scroll or position the insertion point (use the keyboard instead).

If you need to verify a specific command or file name, you can temporarily stop recording keystrokes, by choosing Macro ➤ Pause. When you are ready to continue recording the macro, repeat this choice.

Macro Location   By default, macros are stored in the C:\WPWIN\MACROS directory with the extension .WCM. You can change the directory in the Location of Files dialog box. If you do so, you will not need to supply the path name when playing the macro.

See Also   Button Bar, Keyboard Layout, Location of Files, Macro Conversion

MACRO CONVERSION

WordPerfect 5.1 for Windows creates macros that are entirely different in content and format from the WordPerfect 5.1 for DOS macros. Whereas WordPerfect 5.1 for DOS macros record your keystrokes, WordPerfect 5.1 for Windows records the results of your keystrokes. Nearly all functions of WordPerfect 5.1 for Windows have corresponding commands that can be included in macros. WordPerfect 5.1 for DOS macros required the use of the Macro Editor, while the Windows version allows you to edit macros just like any other document.

The utility program, Macro Facility, provides a conversion routine that will convert WordPerfect 5.1 for DOS macros (.WPM) into WordPerfect 5.1 for Windows format (.WCM).

To Convert a WordPerfect 5.1 Macro to WordPerfect for Windows

If you have just run a macro, the Macro Facility program is preloaded and is listed in the Windows Task List. To access the Macro Facility from the Task List:

1. Press Ctrl+Esc to display the Task List.

2. Double-click on WordPerfect Macro Facility in the displayed list, or highlight it and press ↵.

3. Choose Convert from the Macro Facility's Macro menu.

4. Use the Convert Macro dialog box to locate the .WPM file you want to convert.

5. Choose Convert. The conversion program (WPM2WCM.DLL) must be available to WordPerfect.

If you have not run a macro recently, you can still reach the Macro Facility through the Windows Program Manager:

1. Click the minimize button to reduce WordPerfect to an icon and display Windows Program Manager window.

2. Choose File ➤ Run, type **MFWIN.EXE**, and click Run.

3. Proceed as in steps 3–5 above.

MARGINS

You can set the top, bottom, left, or right margins of your document. You can also release the left margin one or more tab stops. The default margin settings are 1 inch.

To Set Margins

You can set the document margins with the Layout menu or with the ruler (for the left and right margins only). To set the margins with the menu:

1. Move the insertion point to the location where you wish to set the margins (see Notes).

2. Choose Layout ➤ Margins (Ctrl+F8).

3. Enter the measurements for the top, bottom, left, and/or right margins (see Notes).

4. Click OK.

The top bar of the ruler display indicates the position of the left and right margins. To set the left or right margin with the ruler:

1. Choose View ➤ Ruler (Alt+Shift+F3) to display the ruler.

2. Click on the left or right margin mark in the Ruler and drag it to the desired margin position. A dotted alignment guide displays the margin position in the document.

3. Release the mouse button to fix the margin.

The new margin remains in effect to the end of the document or until it is reset.

To Release the Margin

A margin release moves the insertion point and any trailing text one tab stop to the left until it reaches the leftmost tab stop. The moved text will overwrite any text to its left. If the insertion point is at a margin, it will move to the screen equivalent of the edge of the paper. A margin release is often used in outlines to move to a higher outline level. To use the margin release:

1. Position the insertion point at the spot where the margin release is to take effect.

2. Choose Layout ➤ Paragraph ➤ Margin Release, or press (Shift+Tab).

To remove a margin release, you must delete the [Mar Rel] code from Reveal Codes.

● **NOTES** Margins are measured from the top, bottom, left, and right edges of the paper. The measurements are in inches unless you specify a different measurement with the Units of Measure command.

With Auto Code Placement on, the codes are placed at the beginning of the paragraph (for left and right margin settings) or at the top of the page (for top and bottom margin settings). With Auto Code Placement off, the margin setting takes effect starting at the location of the insertion point.

You can change the margins as often as necessary within a document.

To change the left margin or the left and right margins for the current paragraph only, use Indent or Double Indent.

WordPerfect does not usually print text within the top or bottom margin of a page. The First Baseline at Top Margin option of the Typesetting feature will allow you to print a line of text above the top margin. Headers appear immediately below the top margin. Footers and footnotes appear immediately above the bottom margin. If you specify a margin that is less than that which your printer can handle, WordPerfect resets the margin to the printer's minimum setting.

See Also Auto Code Placement, Binding Offset, Indent, Initial Codes, Ruler, Tabs, Units of Measure

MASTER DOCUMENT

Master documents let you create large documents from smaller, more manageable subdocuments. You can combine the subdocuments to create indexes, tables of contents, lists, and other addenda for the master document. Subdocuments are referenced by links in the master document.

To Link a Subdocument to a Master Document

1.   Move the insertion point to the location in the master document where you want to link the subdocument.

2.   Optionally, choose Layout ➤ Page ➤ Page Break, or press Ctrl+↵ to start the subdocument on a new page.

3.   Choose Tools ➤ Master Document ➤ Subdocument.

4.   In the Include Subdocument dialog box, enter the subdocument file name or select a file from the displayed list, and click Include.

To Expand a Master Document

Expanding a master document retrieves the linked subdocuments and places them in their respective link locations.

- Choose Tools ➤ Master Document ➤ Expand Master.

To Condense a Master Document

Condensing a master document removes the linked subdocuments from their link locations.

1.   Choose Tools ➤ Master Document ➤ Condense Master.

2.   If prompted, choose Yes to replace one or more old subdocument files with the subdocuments from the master document, No to condense the master document without saving any edits to its subdocuments, or Cancel.

● **NOTES**   A master document is a large document composed of smaller subdocuments, which are just normal WordPerfect files. Typically, you will edit the subdocuments separately, then use a master document to assemble them.

Subdocument links appear as comments containing *Subdoc:* followed by the path name of the subdocument.

The subdocument need not exist at the time you create the link.

Structuring Master Documents and Subdocuments

The master document should be a skeleton structure for your final document, containing only the following:

- Formatting codes that apply to *all* subdocuments
- Links to each subdocument
- Titles and definitions for endnote location, tables of authorities, tables of contents, indexes, and lists

Subdocuments should contain everything else needed to build the final document, including:

- Text and graphics for each chapter, section, etc.
- Formatting codes specific to each subdocument
- Marked text for cross-references, footnotes, endnotes, tables of authorities, tables of contents, indexes, and lists

Expanding a Master Document

Expanding retrieves subdocuments into the master document. It replaces each "Subdoc: *filename*" comment code with a "Subdoc Start: *filename*" code before and a "Subdoc End: *filename*" code after each retrieved subdocument.

You can edit the text of an expanded master document, including subdocument text.

You must expand a master document before printing, unless you actually want to print the condensed version.

You need not expand a master document before generating lists, tables of contents, and similar items.

Condensing a Master Document

Condensing removes the text and/or graphics of subdocuments within the master document, but retains the links.

See Also

Codes, Cross-Reference, Document Comments, Exit, Footnotes and Endnotes, Generate, Index, Lists, Save Documents, Table of Authorities, Table of Contents

MENUS

WordPerfect for Windows uses the standard Windows Common User Access (CUA) conventions—pull-down menus, dialog boxes, buttons, and scroll bars—to provide access to its features. This entry discusses the use of pull-down menus and the available keystroke alternatives to the various elements of the CUA.

To Choose Menu Options

You can use either the mouse or keyboard to access options (commands) on the menus.

To use the mouse to choose a menu option:

1. Click on the menu name.

2. Move the mouse pointer to the desired option.

3. Click on the option.

4. Repeat steps 2 and 3 for any submenus.

To use the keyboard to select a menu option:

• Press the Alt key and press the underlined letter of the option you want.

Or...

1. Press, then release the Alt key to make the menu bar available.

2. Use the arrow keys to highlight the option you want to choose. Press ↑ or ↓ to move *within* a menu. Press ← or → to move *across* the menu bar.

3. Press ↵ when the option you want is highlighted.

To Cancel a Menu Choice

If you inadvertently choose the wrong menu option you can "back out" from the selection by using one of the following methods:

- Click the menu name or any empty space outside the menu.

- Press and release the Alt key, the F10 key, or the Escape (Esc) key.

● NOTES

Menu Symbols   Table 10 describes some of the symbols that appear next to some menu options.

Shortcut Keystrokes   To use shortcut keystrokes, hold down the first key while pressing the second. For example, to press Shift+F4, hold down the Shift key, press the F4 key, and then release both keys.

Table 10: Symbols used on pull-down menus

Symbol	Meaning
... (ellipses)	Choosing the menu option will take you to a dialog box
Dimmed (grayed)	A dimmed option is currently unavailable
Check mark (✓)	Indicates that an option is currently active ("on")
Triangle (➤)	Leads to another submenu of additional commands
Shortcut key	Indicates a shortcut key (such as **F4**) or keystroke combination (such as **Shift+F4**) that you can use instead of choosing menu options

• **EXAMPLE** When you encounter an instruction involving a series of menu choices and an optional shortcut, such as: Choose **F**ile ➤ **P**rint ➤ **B**inding Offset (F5,B). You can perform the action by any of the following methods:

- Using the left mouse button, click on File, then click on Print, and then click on Binding Offset.

- Press and release the Alt key, and then type the letters F, P, and B (using uppercase or lowercase letters).

- Press and release the Alt key, use the arrow keys to highlight File, and press ↵; use the arrow keys to highlight Print, and press ↵; use Tab to highlight Binding Offset.

- Press the F5 key, and then type the letter B (either uppercase or lowercase).

See Also Cancel, Dialog Boxes, Exit, Help, Menu Setup, Windows

MENU SETUP

WordPerfect uses the standard Windows menu display features. You have the option to display all menu items or to shorten the list of menu items to display only commonly used options.

To display short or full menus, toggle the Short Menus option in the View menu. If a check mark appears in front of the Short Menus item, the list of menu options is shortened. If no check mark is displayed, you will see the full menu.

See Also Menus

MERGE OPERATIONS

Merge operations combine information from two or more sources into a single document. Merge is commonly used to print form letters where the text of the letter remains the same but the name and address information changes for each letter.

To perform a merge, you create a primary file of standard information (e.g., a form letter) and a secondary file of variable information (e.g., names and addresses), and then you merge them into a new document.

To Insert a Merge Command
into a Primary or Secondary File

The primary file contains the standard, unchanging information. The secondary file contains the variable information that will be merged with each copy of the primary file.

To insert a merge command in either type of file:

1. Position the insertion point where you want the merge command.

2. Choose Tools ➤ Merge (Ctrl+F12).

3. Choose a merge command and answer any prompts (see Merge Commands).

To Perform a Merge

Once the primary and secondary files are complete and saved, you may merge the two:

1. Double-click on the document window Control-menu box (or choose File ➤ Close) to clear the document window, if necessary.

2. Choose Tools ➤ Merge ➤ Merge (Ctrl+F12,M).

3. Enter the primary file name. or click the list button to the right of the text box and select a file from the list.

4. Enter the secondary file name or select from the list.

5. Choose OK.

● MERGE COMMANDS

There are dozens of merge programming commands that manage the merge operation's user interface, flow control, merge or subroutine termination, external condition handling, macro execution, variables, system variables, secondary commands execution control, and programming aids. The more commonly used commands are available through menu selection (choose Tools ➤ Merge and then select from the submenu), while the remainder can be selected from the Insert Merge Codes dialog box list.

The commands described below are inserted by means of choosing Tools ➤ Merge (Ctrl+F12). Most of these commands are used in primary files, except End Field, End Record, and Merge Codes ➤ {FIELD NAMES}, which are used in secondary files.

End Field (Alt+Enter)	Ends the field and automatically inserts a hard return [HRt] code into the secondary file.
End Record (Alt+Shift+Enter)	Ends a record and automatically inserts a hard page break [HPg] into the secondary file.
Field	Inserts the contents of a field into the merged document. Enter the field number or field name.
Input	Prompts for keyboard input during a merge. Enter a prompt message (e.g., "donation amount"), and then press Alt+Enter.
Page Off	Eliminates the automatic hard page break [HPg] between copies of the primary file in the merged document.

Next Record	Moves the record pointer in the secondary file to the next record during a merge. This command is used with other merge programming language commands.
Merge Codes	Displays a list of available merge commands and lets you insert any merge command, including advanced programming language commands, into a merge file. Highlight the command you want, press ↵, then respond to any prompts.
Convert	Converts old merge codes (from versions before WordPerfect 5.0) to WordPerfect for Windows format.
Merge	Performs the merge operation. Enter primary and secondary file names.

● NOTES

Primary Files   A *primary file* is required for each merge. This file contains standard text, graphics, and formatting information; field names or numbers indicating where to insert data; and, optionally, other merge commands.

During a merge, information from the secondary file, keyboard, or DOS delimited text file is substituted into the appropriate fields of the primary file, and the file is formatted automatically.

To insert a field to be substituted during the merge, choose Tools ➤ Merge ➤ Field (Ctrl+F12,F), then enter the field name or number and choose OK.

To insert a message that will request input from the keyboard, choose Tools ➤ Merge ➤ Input (Ctrl+F12,I), then enter the message prompting the user for data and choose OK.

Secondary Files   The *secondary file* contains the data to be inserted into the primary file. This file contains *records*, each of which is divided into one or more *fields*. Fields are always numbered from top to bottom within a record. You can assign a field name to each field using the {FIELD NAMES} command.

The primary file can insert and reuse these fields in any order, and need not use every field defined in the secondary file.

Before merging, you can sort the secondary file or select certain records from it.

Defining Field Names in Secondary Files   To reference field *names* instead of *numbers* in your primary file, follow these steps:

1. Move the insertion point to the top of the secondary file.
2. Choose Tools ➤ Merge ➤ Merge Codes (Ctrl+F12,C).
3. Choose {FIELD NAMES} and click Insert.
4. Enter a name for a field.
5. Choose Add.
6. To add other field names, click on the Field Name text bar and repeat steps 4–5, as needed.
7. Click OK when done.
8. Choose Close to return to the document.

Inserting Fields and Records into Secondary Files
Each secondary file record must contain the same number of fields, and each field of the same type must either contain the same kind of information or remain empty. However, you need not keep the same number of words or lines within each field.

To insert a field into a secondary file, type the field information at the appropriate spot in each record and then choose Tools ➤ Merge ➤ End Field (Alt+↵). This inserts {END FIELD} followed by a hard return [HRt].

To insert an empty field, press End Field (Alt+↵) at the beginning of a line.

Repeat this process for each field in a record, then insert an End of Record code {END RECORD} by choosing **Tools** ➤ **Merge** ➤ End Record (Alt+Shift+↵). Records are separated by a hard page break.

Continue inserting fields and records until your secondary file is complete.

Do not insert extra spaces or hard returns (↵) before or after the {END FIELD} or {END RECORD}.

Defining Default Field and Record Start and End Characters

The secondary file can contain delimited DOS text format data, such as that exported from spreadsheet and database files. Before merging such a file, you must define the field and record delimiters.

To define *default* delimiters before merging:

1. Choose **File** ➤ **Preferences** ➤ **Merge**.

2. Position the insertion point at the desired text box (use Tab and Shift+Tab).

3. Click the pop-up menu arrow and select desired option: Tab, Line Feed, Form Feed, or Carriage Return.

4. Repeat step 3 as necessary to define all delimiters.

To define delimiters when you begin the merge:

1. Choose **Tools** ➤ **Merge** ➤ **Merge** (Ctrl+F12,M).

2. Type names of primary and secondary files (or click the list button to the right of the text box to select a file.)

3. Check the ASCII Delimited Text (DOS) check box.

4. Choose OK.

5. Enter beginning and ending delimiters for fields and records.

6. Choose OK.

Interacting with a Merge   If you used an Input command in your primary file, the merge will pause, display the message you entered, and wait for keyboard input. Respond by typing the required data, and then press End Field (Alt+⏎) to continue the merge.

To stop a merge, press Escape (Esc); to cancel the merge after a {CANCEL OFF} command, press Ctrl+Break.

● **EXAMPLE**   Figures 10 through 12 show a sample form letter (primary file), the customer information list (secondary file), and a sample of a merged form letter.

See Also   File Manager, Graphics and Graphic Boxes, Initial Codes, Sorting and Selecting

---

Acme Furniture
P.O. Box 1234
Los Angeles, CA 91234

August 11, 1991

{FIELD}First Name~ {FIELD}Last Name~
{FIELD}Address~
{FIELD}City~, {FIELD}State~ {FIELD}Zip~

Dear {FIELD}Salutation~:

Just a quick note to remind you that our annual clearance sale is happening next weekend at the Los Angeles Civic Center.

As usual, prices will be slashed below *our* production costs, so don't miss this important event.

Hope to see you there!

Best Regards:

Jason Klemmer
Vice President

Figure 10: A primary file (form letter)

MOUSE

The mouse provides a means of navigating through the Word-Perfect graphical user interface. You can use the mouse to select text, move the insertion point, select options from menus and dialog boxes, and operate on graphics boxes. These operations can also be performed using the keyboard.

To Select Text

To select text for cut and paste, changing fonts, or other operations:

1. Position the insertion point at the beginning of the text.

2. Press the left mouse button.

```
{FIELD NAMES}
     First Name¯
     Last Name¯
     Address¯
     City¯
     State¯
     Zip¯
     Salutation¯¯
{END RECORD}
===============================================================
Frank{END FIELD}
Fleinder{END FIELD}
123 Oak St.{END FIELD}
Glendora{END FIELD}
KS{END FIELD}
54321{END FIELD}
Frank{END FIELD}
{END RECORD}
===============================================================
Nita{END FIELD}
Bonita{END FIELD}
P.O. Box 5432{END FIELD}
Glendora{END FIELD}
KS{END FIELD}
54320{END FIELD}
Miss Bonita{END FIELD}
{END RECORD}
===============================================================
Jane{END FIELD}
Tarzana{END FIELD}
555 Apple St.{END FIELD}
Jackson{END FIELD}
KS{END FIELD}
54300{END FIELD}
Jane{END FIELD}
{END RECORD}
===============================================================
```

Figure 11: A secondary file (customer information)

3.   Hold the button down and drag the mouse pointer.

4.   Release the mouse button. The text the mouse pointer passes over will be highlighted.

To deselect the text, click the left mouse button again.

You can also double-click to select the current word, triple-click to select the sentence, and quadruple-click to select the paragraph.

To Move the Insertion Point

Move the mouse pointer (usually an I beam) to the desired location and click the mouse button. If the location you want is off the screen,

---

Acme Furniture
P.O. Box 1234
Los Angeles, CA 91234

August 11, 1991

Frank Fleinder
123 Oak St.
Glendora, KS 54321

Dear Frank:

Just a quick note to remind you that our annual clearance sale is happening next weekend at the Los Angeles Civic Center.

As usual, prices will be slashed below *our* production costs, so don't miss this important event.

Hope to see you there!

Best Regards:

Jason Klemmer
Vice President

Figure 12: A merged form letter

point to the up or down arrow in the scroll bar and hold down the mouse button, or drag the scroll box down the scroll bar.

To move the insertion point to an inactive window, click on any part of the window. The window will be activated.

To Choose Menu Options

You can use the mouse to choose menu items, select items from list boxes, and turn check box options on and off. You can use the mouse alone or in combination with keystrokes.

To choose menu items, click on the menu name and then click on the item you want, or click on the menu name, drag the mouse to the item you want, and then release the button.

To make a selection from a list box, double-click the item or click the item and choose the default button (the one with the dark outline).

To turn a check box item on or off, move the mouse pointer to the square and click the mouse button.

Radio buttons provide mutually exclusive alternatives; you can select only one at a time. Click on a button to select it.

To Control Graphic Boxes

You can use the mouse to select, move, or size any graphic box. Select the box by clicking anywhere in the box. Deselect it by clicking outside the box.

To move a graphics box, select the box and drag it to the new location.

To size a box, select the box, then drag one of the squares along the box border ("handles") to achieve the desired size.

You can access the Text, Figure, or Equation Editor that was used when you created the box by double-clicking anywhere in the box.

• **NOTES**   Before using the mouse, you must properly install it as defined in your documentation, and then set up the mouse for use with Windows. You can customize your mouse through the Windows Control Panel by changing the double-click speed, switching left and right button functions, and changing the speed of movement. It's a good idea to jot down current settings and consult your mouse manual before changing any mouse settings.

In WordPerfect, always click the left mouse button, unless otherwise directed (or you have switched the left and right button functions).

Mouse Terms   Some commonly used mouse terms are:

Click	Press the button and release immediately.
Double-click	Click the button two times quickly.
Drag	Press the button and hold it down while moving the mouse.

Be sure not to move the mouse while multiple-clicking.

See Also   Dialog Boxes, Equations, Graphics and Graphic Boxes, Menus

MOVE

Move operations let you move, copy, delete, and paste selected text, tabular columns, or rectangles of text within your document and between WordPerfect documents. For information on moving data into a document from a file in another Windows application that supports Dynamic Data Exchange (DDE), or from one of the DOS spreadsheets that supports the Spreadsheet Link feature, see the DDE Link and Spreadsheet Link command references.

To Move or Copy Selected Text

1. Select the text you want to move or copy (see Notes).

2. To cut text, choose Edit ➤ Cut (Shift+Del). To copy text, select Edit ➤ Copy (Ctrl+Ins). Cut removes the text from its original position; Copy leaves the original text intact.

3. Move the insertion point to the location where you want text to appear and choose Edit ➤ Paste (Shift+Ins).

To move text to another WordPerfect document:

1. With both files open, repeat steps 1 and 2 above.

2. Activate the document window of the file into which the text will be inserted.

3. Position the insertion point at the desired location.

4. Choose Edit ➤ Paste (Shift+Ins).

To cut or copy several segments of text within your document to another document, you can use Append. Append adds the selected text to the Clipboard without erasing its previous contents. When you are ready, the segments can all be pasted at once. Append is not available for tabular columns and rectangular text.

To Work with Columns or Rectangles

You can rearrange columns created with Tabs or Indents, and rectangular text.

To work with tabular columns:

1. Position the insertion point at the first character after the Tab code in the first column you want to select.

2. Drag the insertion point to the opposite corner (i.e., the last row of the rightmost column) you want to select.

3. Choose Edit ➤ Select.

4.   Choose **Tabular Column.**

5.   Choose **Edit ➤ Cut** (or **Copy**).

6.   Move the insertion point to the location where the text should appear and choose **Edit ➤ Paste.**

Rectangular text consists of lines ending in hard returns. You select it by positioning the insertion point at one corner and dragging diagonally to the opposite corner. Choose **Rectangle** in step 4 above and repeat steps 5 and 6.

● NOTES   Move options let you rearrange and copy text without retyping. When you cut, copy, or append, the selected text is written to the Clipboard and remains there until the next Cut or Copy operation.

In addition to the menu choices, you can select specific portions of text with the mouse:

- To select the current word, double-click the mouse.

- To select the current sentence, triple-click the mouse.

- To select the current paragraph, quadruple-click the mouse.

See Also   Append, Cut and Paste, Delete Operations, Retrieve, Selecting Text, Undelete

NETWORK

Running WordPerfect for Windows on a network offers some advantages in the sharing of information and peripheral equipment, such as printers.

To Use a Network Printer

To use a network printer, you must connect to it by using the Windows Control Panel window. See your Windows reference for details. After you have made the connection, you can choose File ➤ Select Printer to setup the printer. Passwords may be required to access the network for printing; see the Password command reference.

OUTLINE

Outlining lets you automatically number entries (paragraphs) and create hierarchical structures that can easily be rearranged. You can create different outline styles or change an existing outline style. WordPerfect automatically renumbers your outline to reflect changes.

To Create an Outline

To create an outline:

1. Move the insertion point to the location where outline should begin.

2. Choose Tools ➤ Outline ➤ Outline On. The word *Outline* appears in the status line.

3. Press ↵ to insert the first-level entry number.

4. Enter text for first-level entry.

5. To add another entry:

- For an entry at the same level, press ↵.

- For an entry at a subordinate level (e.g., to move from level 1 to level 2), press ↵, and then press Tab once for each level.

- For an entry at a higher level (e.g., to move from level 2 back to level 1), press ↵, and then choose Layout ➤ Paragraph ➤ Margin Release, or press Shift+Tab, once for each level.

6. Repeat steps 4 and 5 as desired.

7. Choose Tools ➤ Outline ➤ Outline Off when done.

To insert blank lines between levels, press ↵ once for each blank line.

To Define the Outline Style

You can change the numbering system for your outline and save it in the directory of styles. The new style takes effect at the position of the insertion point. If you save the style, you can use it in later documents.

1. Move the insertion point to the location where the style should take effect.

2. Choose Tools ➤ Outline ➤ Define (Alt+Shift+F5).

3. Define the outline numbering style and options (see Options).

4. Click OK until you return to the document window.

To Move, Copy, or Delete an Outline Family

An outline family consists of the paragraph number and text at the location of the insertion point plus the numbers and text of any subordinate paragraphs. You can move or copy the family to a new location, or delete it entirely.

1. Position the insertion point at the top level of the family.

2. Choose Tools ➤ Outline.

3. Choose Move Family, Copy Family, or Delete Family.

4. For Move or Copy Family, move the insertion point to the spot where the family should appear and press ↵. For Delete Family, choose Yes to confirm the deletion.

The paragraphs numbers that are displaced are automatically renumbered.

● OPTIONS

Paragraph (pre-defined format)	Sets numbering style to 1. a. i. (1) (a) (i) 1) a).
Outline (pre-defined format)	Sets numbering style to I. A. 1. a. (1) (a) i) a).
Legal (pre-defined format)	Sets numbering style to 1 .1 .1 .1 .1 .1 .1 .1 (numbers are attached to the previous level, as in 1.4.1).
Bullets (pre-defined format)	Sets numbering style to
	● ● _ ■ ✻ ✦ ▬ ✖
User-defined	Lets you define numbering styles for each level. For each level, choose: **1** (digits); **A** (uppercase letters); **a** (lowercase letters); **I** (uppercase Roman); **i** (lowercase Roman); **X** (uppercase Roman with digits, if attached; e.g., II., 2.I, 2.1.I); **x** (lowercase Roman with digits, if attached; e.g., ii., 2.i, 2.1.i); or any other character or punctuation, including special characters.
Attach Previous Level	Lets you attach one level to the previous level number. Check box to attach the level to the previous level number (e.g., *I.A.* and *1.A.1.*), or leave blank to leave it unattached (e.g., *A.* and *1.*).
Starting Outline Number	Sets the starting paragraph number at any level. Enter the starting level number in *numeric* format; separate the levels with a space, period, or comma (e.g., type 6.2.3 to start Outline style numbering at level VI.B.3).

Current Outline Style	Leave the default **No** Style or choose **Change**. If you choose Change, highlight the Outline Style name you want and choose **Select**.
Enter Inserts Paragraph Number	Leave the box checked to automatically insert a paragraph number when you press ↵ after typing paragraph text, or leave it blank to have ↵ simply end a line. If you turn this option off, you must use Paragraph Numbering to insert paragraph numbers.
Auto Adjust to Current Level	Leave the box checked to insert new paragraph numbers at the same level as the previous paragraph number, or toggle it off to always insert new paragraphs at level 1. (This has no effect on paragraph numbers outside of outlines.)
Outline **On**	Leave the box checked to begin typing an outline, or uncheck the box to return to the document window.

● **NOTES**   An outline entry is a paragraph; the terms are synonymous because an entry is defined by its ending hard return. WordPerfect also offers paragraph numbering. Like outlining, it lets you define up to 8 numbering levels, and both automatically assign and update numbers to reflect editing changes. Unlike outlining, it lets you number paragraphs in a document manually and fix a paragraph's numbering level. They also differ in that an outline is generally intended to be the "skeleton" of a document, whereas paragraph numbering can be used in any document.

See Also   Indent, Initial Codes, Paragraph Numbering, Special Characters, Styles, Tabs

OVERSTRIKE

The Overstrike command lets you print two or more characters on top of one another to create special characters not normally available on your printer.

To Create an Overstrike

1. Move the insertion point to the location where you want the overstrike.

2. Choose Font ➤ Overstrike ➤ Create.

3. In the Create/Edit Overstrike dialog box, assign any font attributes before entering the overstrike characters, by clicking on the arrow button and selecting from the list. Attribute codes will appear in the text box, with the insertion point between them. Enter the characters and choose OK.

To Edit an Overstrike

1. Move the insertion point to the right of an existing overstrike combination.

2. Choose Font ➤ Overstrike ➤ Edit.

3. Edit the overstrike combination and press ↵.

• **NOTES**   Overstruck characters are printed one over the other, without advancing the print head (e.g., **0/** prints a zero with a slash through it, Ø). The overstrike characters may include Font attributes (e.g., Bold, Underline, Italics).

Overstrike character combinations available through WordPerfect's special character sets should be entered with Font ➤ WP Characters (Ctrl+W), rather than with Overstrike.

See Also   Codes, Font Attributes, Special Characters

PAGE BREAKS

The Page Break command lets you end a page (insert a page break) anywhere in a document. WordPerfect automatically inserts a soft page break code [SPg] when you reach the bottom margin of a page. The soft page break appears on-screen as a single solid line.

When you manually insert a page break, a hard page break code [HPg] is inserted at the insertion point. This hard page break remains at the end of the page regardless of any additions or deletions you make to the preceding text. Hard page breaks are displayed on-screen as a double solid line across the page.

To Insert a Page Break

1. Position the insertion point where you want the page to break.

2. Choose Layout ➤ Page ➤ Page Break (Alt+F9,P), or press Ctrl+↵.

To Keep a Block of Text on One Page

1. Select the text you want to keep together on the page. The block cannot overlap pages separated by a hard page break.

2. Choose Layout ➤ Page ➤ Block Protect (Alt+F9,B). A Block Protect code [Block Pro:On] is inserted into your document at the beginning of the selected text, and a [Block Pro:Off] code is inserted at the end of the selected text.

To Insert a Conditional End of Page

With a conditional end of page, you specify a number of lines to be kept together on a page, such as a heading and its following paragraph.

Unlike a Block Protect selection, this number of lines remains fixed regardless of the changes you make within it.

1. Position the insertion point just above the lines you want to keep together.

2. Choose Layout ➤ Page ➤ Conditional End of Page (Alt+F9,E).

3. Enter the number of lines to keep together.

4. Click OK. A Conditional End of Page code [Cndl EOP:] is inserted in your document.

● NOTES   You can delete hard page break codes [HPg] and codes that prevent page breaks. To delete these codes, choose View ➤ Reveal Codes (Alt+F3), click on the code you want to delete, and press the Delete key. You cannot delete soft page break codes [SPg].

A hard page break is also used to end one column and move to the next.

See Also   Page Numbering, Page Suppress, Selecting Text, Widow/Orphan

PAGE NUMBERING

The Page Numbering command lets you specify the type of page numbering you want and where the number is printed on the page. You can also set the page number, add preceding or trailing text, and insert a page number within the text.

To Start Page Numbering

1. Choose Layout ➤ Page ➤ Numbering (Alt+F9,N).

2. Select **P**osition and indicate the location for the page numbers: **N**o Page Numbering, Top **L**eft, Top **C**enter, Top **R**ight, **A**lternating Top, **B**ottom Left, Bo**t**tom Center, Bottom Right, or Al**t**ernating Bottom.

3. Choose one or more page number options and answer any prompts (see Options).

4. Click OK.

● **OPTIONS**   In addition to Position, you can choose the following options from the Page Numbering dialog box.

Numbering **T**ype	Click on the button and drag the highlight to select the page number style you want: Arabic (**1**, 2, 3, 4…), Roman lowercase (i, ii, iii, **iv**…), or Roman uppercase (**I**, II, III, IV…).
New Page Number	Enter the number you want to appear on the current page, if it is different from the assigned number.
Accompanying Text	Type the text you wish to appear before or after the page number. For example, if you want the word "Page" to precede the page number, type **Page** before the number code ([^B]) in the text box.
Insert Page Number	Click this button to insert the current page number at the insertion point. You can insert the page number in the document window, headers, footers, endnotes, and footnotes.
Force Current Page	Choose **O**dd to ensure that the current page will always be numbered with an odd number, or **E**ven to ensure that it will always be numbered with an even number.

• **NOTES** WordPerfect numbers your document pages only if you request it. Page numbers are displayed only when the document is printed or is previewed using the Print Preview command. Use the Page Suppress command to prevent the printing of a number on a particular page without interrupting the numbering sequence.

If Auto Code Placement is off, you must insert the page numbering code at the beginning of the page. Otherwise, page numbering will start on the next page.

To invoke page numbering automatically in all documents, insert a page numbering code in the Initial Codes.

To include page numbers in headers or footers, click the Page Number button in the header or footer editor.

See Also Headers and Footers, Initial Codes, Page Suppress, Print Preview

PAGE SUPPRESS

The Page Suppress command prevents the printing of page numbers, as well as headers or footers, on a single page without interrupting the page number sequence. It also gives you the option of printing the page number at the bottom center on the current page.

To Suppress Numbering on the Current Page Only

1. Position the insertion point at the beginning of the page on which you don't want a page number, headers, or footers.

2. Choose Layout ➤ Page ➤ Suppress (Alt+F9,U).

3. Indicate the element that you don't want to print: **H**eader A, **H**eader B, **F**ooter A, **F**ooter B, or **P**age Numbers. If you do not opt to suppress page numbers, you can choose to Print Page **N**umber at Bottom Center of this page only.

4. Click OK when done.

See Also   Headers and Footers, Initial Codes, Page Numbering

PAPER SIZE

The Paper Size dialog box enables you to select a paper size and type to use when printing the current document. You can also create customized paper size definitions and delete old ones from the list of sizes. Use these custom definitions to select double-sided printing or landscape orientation for all or part of a document.

To use the Paper Size dialog box, you must have WordPerfect printer drivers installed and selected in the Select Printer dialog box.

To Choose a Paper Size

1. Position the insertion point before any text at the top of the page where the paper size should take effect.

2. Choose Layout ➤ **P**age ➤ Paper **S**ize (Alt+F9,S). The Paper Size dialog box will appear.

3. Highlight the paper size you want and choose **S**elect. If the paper size you need is not on the list, you can create it by following the steps in the next section.

To Add or Edit a Paper Size Definition

1. Choose Layout ➤ **P**age ➤ Paper **S**ize ➤ **A**dd (Alt+F9,SA) or Layout ➤ **P**age ➤ Paper **S**ize ➤ **E**dit (Alt+F9,SE).

2. Modify the paper size definition using the selections listed below.

3. Click OK to return to the Paper Size menu.

Use the following selections to define the paper size:

Paper **T**ype	Choose a paper type from the list of various paper types (e.g., standard, bond, envelope, labels), or name your own paper type.
Paper **S**ize	Choose a paper size from the list of various page sizes, or choose Other to enter a custom size. The default paper size is 8½ inches by 11 inches.
Text Adjustments	If your printer is not positioning a document on the paper correctly, you can adjust it vertically (To**p**) or horizontally (Sid**e**). Enter the distance you want to adjust the text in each direction. This option may require some trial-and-error.
Paper **O**rientation	Use this box if you need to print in landscape orientation (or return to portrait orientation). Icons display the four possible combinations of paper and font orientation. Select by clicking either an icon or check boxes.
Paper Lo**c**ation	Choose **M**anual, **C**ontinuous (for tractor-fed paper), or **B**in (for bin-fed paper). If you choose Bin, you must enter a bin number.
P**r**ompt to Load Paper	Select this check box to have WordPerfect notify you when you need to load paper.
Double Sided Printing	Check the box if your printer can print on both sides, or leave it blank if it cannot.
Binding Edge	A *binding edge* is extra space added to the top or left edge of the page to allow room for binding. Choose **T**op or **L**eft to add the binding offset at the top or the left edge of the page, respectively.

Labels   Click on the button to open the Edit
                          Labels dialog box (see "To Create
                          Labels").

You only need to use Paper Size for non-standard forms, such as
envelopes, labels, or letterhead.

When you select a paper size, WordPerfect inserts a code like the
following: [Paper Sz/Typ:8.5" × 14", Legal].

Definitions are printer specific. Once you create a definition for a
specific printer, you can choose it as needed and don't have to
redefine it.

If necessary, you can insert more than one paper size code in your
document. During printing, WordPerfect looks at the printer's list
of paper sizes and types and uses the matching definition. If it can't
find an exact match, it uses the [ALL OTHERS] definition. You can
select this definition manually if you expect to print the document
on more than one printer.

To Copy or Delete a Paper Size Definition

1.   Choose Layout ➤ Page ➤ Paper Size (Alt+F9,S).

2.   Highlight the paper size you want to copy or delete.

3.   Choose Copy or Delete.

4.   When you choose Copy, the Add Paper Size dialog box
          appears. Edit the paper size definition and name the new
          paper type. Choose OK.

5.   When you choose Delete, the "Delete *selected paper* defini-
          tion?" message appears. Choose Yes.

6.   To exit the dialog box without selecting a Page Size option,
          click the Close button.

To Create Labels

1. Choose Layout ➤ Page ➤ Paper Size ➤ Add ➤ Labels (Alt+F9,SAL).

2. Create the label definition using the selctions listed below.

3. Click OK until you're back at the Paper Size dialog box, highlight the labels definition, and choose Select.

Use the following selections in creating the labels definition:

Label Size	Enter the **W**idth and **H**eight of an individual label.
Labels Per Page	Enter the number of **C**olumns and **R**ows of labels on each labels sheet.
Top Left Label	Enter the distance from the **T**op and **L**eft edge of the page for the first label.
Distance between Labels	Enter the distance between the **C**olumns and **R**ows of labels.
Label Margins	Enter the **L**eft, **R**ight, To**p**, and **B**ottom margin for each label.
Remove Labels	Select this to remove the highlighted label from the list.

● NOTES   Place Paper Size definitions in the document Initial Codes to avoid printing only one entry per page of labels.

When typing the text of your labels, choose Layout ➤ Page ➤ Page Break (Ctrl+↵) to separate each label.

See Also   Binding Offset, Initial Codes, Macros, Print, Printer Select, Units of Measure

PARAGRAPH NUMBERING

The Paragraph Numbering command numbers paragraphs one at a time, without requiring you to turn outlining on and off. It's also useful for "fixing" a paragraph number at a specific level. You can use paragraph numbering inside or outside of an outline.

For details on creating outlines and specifying numbering styles, see the Outline command reference.

Paragraph numbers are separated by levels. The maximum number of levels is eight.

To Number Paragraphs

1. Position the insertion point at the spot where the paragraph number should appear.

2. Choose **T**ools ➤ Outline ➤ Paragraph Number (Alt+F5).

3. To number your paragraphs automatically, choose **A**uto. If you want to control the numbering level, choose **M**anual and enter a level number (1–8).

4. Choose Insert.

To Change a Paragraph's Level Number

- To increase the level of an automatic paragraph number outside of an outline, move the insertion point to the immediate left of an existing paragraph number and press *Tab*, or choose **L**ayout ➤ Paragraph ➤ Indent (F7).

- To decrease the level, move the insertion point to the immediate left of an existing paragraph number and choose **L**ayout ➤ Paragraph ➤ **M**argin Release (Shift+Tab), or press the Backspace key.

You cannot change the level of a fixed paragraph number outside of an outline. See the Outline command reference for information on changing paragraph levels within an outline.

● **NOTES**   Automatic paragraph numbering inserts paragraph numbers according to the settings in the Define Paragraph Numbering dialog box.

To delete a paragraph number, move the insertion point to the number, and then press the *Delete* key.

If Auto Code Placement is on, the paragraph number code [Par Num:Auto] is inserted at the beginning of the paragraph.

See Also   Indent, Outline, Tabs

PASSWORD

You can add passwords to your documents to protect them from being accessed by others. A password-protected document cannot be retrieved or printed unless the correct password is entered.

To Add or Change a Password

1. Open the document.
2. Choose File ➤ Password.
3. Type the password and click Set. You can enter a maximum of 23 characters. The password will not appear on the screen.
4. Re-enter the password for verification and click Set again.
5. Save the file and close it to activate the password.

To Remove a Password

1.   Open the document. The File Password Protected dialog
         box asks for the password. Supply it and choose OK.

2.   Choose File ➤ Password.

3.   Type in the password and click Remove.

4.   Save the file.

● **NOTES**   If a file has been saved with a password, WordPerfect
will request the password if you use the File Manager to print,
retrieve, merge, sort, or access that file.

Passwords do not protect the file from being deleted, nor do they
provide high-level security or encryption.

See Also   Exit, File Manager, Retrieve, Save Document

PREFERENCES

The Preferences command lets you customize WordPerfect for your
hardware and work preferences. These settings affect all Word-
Perfect users and remain in effect whenever you use WordPerfect,
until you change them.

To Set Your Work Preferences

1.   Choose File ➤ Preferences.

2.   Choose one or more options (see Options).

3.   Click OK until you return to the document window.

● OPTIONS

Location of Files	Sets the default location for file categories (documents, graphics, macros, etc.) and directories (style, main, etc.). You can also click on the Select File Button which displays a menu of file names within the path or lets you change directories and drives. See the Location of Files command reference.
Backup	Controls automatic backups. See the Backup command reference.
Environment	Lets you change the working environment settings, such as beep options, ruler, and hyphenation. See the Environment command reference.
Display	Selects and controls the appearance of screen displays. See the Display command reference.
Print	Controls the print options, such as the number of copies, quality settings, text marking (redlining) and font size defaults. See the Print command reference.
Keyboard	Selects and customizes your keyboard. See the Keyboard Layout command reference.
Initial Codes	Defines the initial format settings for documents. See the Initial Codes command reference.
Document Summary	Lets you create or print a document summary, which includes a document reference and description. See the Document Summary command reference.
Date Format	Controls the format for dates and times. See the Date/Time Operations command reference.
Merge	Sets the default merge delimiters for DOS text files. See the Merge Operations command reference.

| Table of Authorities | Sets default appearance for tables of authorities. See the Table of Authorities command reference. |
| Equations | Sets the default appearance for Equations. See the Equations command reference. |

PRINT

The Print dialog box lets you control all the options associated with printing a document. You can print all or selected parts of a document that is open in a window or stored on disk. You can also save the print output to a disk for printing at a later time or from another computer.

To Print an Entire Document

1. Choose File ➤ Print ➤ Full Document (F5,F).

2. Select Print.

3. While the document is printing, a window shows the status of the print job.

To Print the Current Page

1. Choose File ➤ Print ➤ Current Page (F5,C).

2. Select Print.

3. While the current page is printing, a window shows the status of the print job.

To Print Selected Text

1. Select the text you want to print.

2. Choose File ➤ Print ➤ Selected Text (F5,L).

3. Select Print.

4. While the selected text is printing, a window shows the status of the print job.

To Print Multiple Pages

1. Choose File ➤ Print ➤ Multiple Pages (F5,M).

2. Select Print.

3. Choose the options you want from the dialog box. Table 12 shows how to specify groups of pages.

Print **R**ange	Enter the starting and ending page numbers. The default is [ALL].
Odd/Even Pages	Drag the mouse to choose one of the five options: **N**one, **O**dd, **E**ven, Lo**g**ical (label) Odd or Lo**g**ical (label) Even.
Document Summary	Click on the box if you also want to print the document summary.

3. Select **P**rint.

Table 11: Specifying multiple pages for printing

Type	To Print
n	Page number ,n where *n* is an Arabic or Roman page number.
n–m	Pages *n* through *m*, where *n* and *m* are Arabic or Roman page numbers.
–m	From the beginning of the document to page *m*.
n–	From page *n* to end of document.
S–	The document summary and the entire document.
x:	Section *x*, where *x* is a section number. You can also follow the section number and colon (:) with an individual page or range of pages (e.g., **3:4-5** to print pages 4 and 5 in section 3).

You must enter the page numbers within a section in numerical order (e.g., **1,3**, *not* **3,1**); otherwise, only the first page specified will print. Similary, you must enter the section numbers in numerical order (e.g., **1:i,1:5,2:ii**, *not* **2:ii,1:i,1:5**); otherwise, only pages in the first specified section will print.

You can use a comma or a space to separate individual pages or ranges from one another.

If you omit the section number, WordPerfect looks for the first page matching the Roman or Arabic page number you entered.

To Print a Document on Disk

1.   Choose File ➤ Print ➤ Document on Disk (F5,D), and then click **Print**.

2.   Enter the name of the file to print or click the File Select button, click the file name, and then click on **Select**.

3.   If you do not want to print the entire document, enter the number of pages to print in the Range text box.

4.   Choose **Odd** or **Even** (or Logical Odd or Logical Even for labels) and Document **Summary**, if you want to print odd pages only, even pages only, or the document summary.

5.   Select **Print**.

To Print Document to Disk

When you print a document to a disk, the document is sent to a file in a DOS file text format for later printing and viewing with the DOS PRINT and TYPE commands on a computer without WordPerfect. It is not sent to the printer. The WordPerfect printer drivers must be selected to print a document to disk.

1.   Choose File ➤ Print ➤ Select (F5,S), or File ➤ Select Printer.

2.   Choose **W**ordPerfect from the Printer Drivers dialog box.

3.   Highlight the printer you want and click on **S**etup to display the Printer Setup dialog box.

4. Choose File from the Port pop-up list.

5. Enter the file name to which the document will be printed. Be sure to include the full path name.

6. Click OK.

7. From the Select Printer dialog box, choose Select to choose the printer.

8. Select Print to print the document to the file.

9. Follow steps 1–6 to change the port back to its original setting.

The DOS text file you created is not an ASCII file. If you have problems printing this file from DOS, use the DOS COPY command with the /b switch instead of the DOS PRINT command.

To Print Multiple Copies

1. Choose File ➤ Print ➤ Number of Copies (F5,N).

2. Click on the up arrow to increase the number of copies, or enter the quantity in the text box.

3. Optionally, toggle the Generated By setting from Word-Perfect to Printer (see Notes).

4. Select Print or Close.

To Change Graphics or Text Quality

1. Choose File ➤ Print ➤ Graphics Quality (F5,G), or File ➤ Print ➤ Text Quality (F5,T).

2. Click on the selection window and drag the mouse to choose High, Medium, Draft, or Do Not Print.

3. Select Print to print the document, or Close to exit the dialog box.

● **NOTES**   Printing takes place in the background, using a temporary copy of your document, so that you may continue working in the document window while the printing takes place.

When printing labels, you can print odd or even *pages* of labels by specifying Odd or Even. You can also print every other label on the page by specifying Logical Odd or Logical Even.

See the Typesetting command reference for information on kerning, printer command, word and letter spacing, justification limits, baseline placement, and leading adjustment.

See the Paper Size command reference for information on defining non-standard paper sizes and types.

When you are printing multiple copies, the second and succeeding copies can be generated by either WordPerfect or the printer. That is, WordPerfect can repeat the information it sends to the printer once for each copy of a page, or it can send the information only once and let the printer's internal software produce the succeeding pages. Choosing Printer is usually faster, but the WordPerfect option provides copies that are already collated.

See Also   Binding Offset, Cartridges and Fonts, Document Summary, Paper Size, Print Preview, Printer Select, Selecting Text, Typesetting

PRINT PREVIEW

The Print Preview command enables you to view a document on-screen before printing. Print Preview displays document text, headers, footers, footnotes, endnotes, line numbers, margins, page numbers, graphics and typesetting features as they will appear on the printed page. The display is formatted for the selected printer (see the Printer Select command reference).

Print Preview also lets you create and edit a Button Bar for customizing icons.

To Preview a Document

1.   Choose File ➤ Print Preview (Shift+F5).

2.   The current page will appear in full-page view in the Preview window. Select a preview option to move around the window or preview specific areas (see Options).

● OPTIONS

File   Print opens the Print dialog box, and closes the Print Preview window.

View   100%: Displays the current page at its actual font size. 200%: Displays the current page at twice its actual size.

Zoom **In**: Increases the view size of the page by 25 percent. You can continue to increase the page size until you reach a maximum of 400 percent. Use the scroll bars on the side and bottom of the screen to view off-screen text and graphics.

Zoom **Out**: Decreases the view size of the page by 25 percent until the full page is displayed.

Zoom Area: Enables you to zoom in on a particular region, at up to 400 percent. Click at opposite corners to define the area. In the zoomed display, clicking anywhere brings up a miniature view of the page you can use to move the zoom area.

Zoom to **F**ull Width: Returns the view of the document to the full width of the page at 100 percent.

Reset: Returns the view of the document to the size and scale selected when the Print Preview window was last closed.

Button Bar: Turns the Button Bar feature on or off. When on, a check mark appears in front of the Button Bar option.

Button Bar **S**etup: Lets you edit the Button Bar. You can reposition the Print Preview Button Bar and/or select what is displayed on the buttons (in text, picture, or both).

Pages   Full Page: Displays the entire page layout.
Facing Pages: Displays two pages—left-facing (even-numbered) and right-facing (odd-numbered) pages. The mouse pointer changes to a magnifying glass, enabling you to select a page and see it in an enlarged view.
Go To Page: Enables you to quickly access a specific page number.
Previous Page: Displays the page preceding the one shown on-screen.
Next Page: Displays the page following the one shown on-screen.

Help   Transfers you to the WordPerfect Help menu (see the Help command reference)

● **NOTES**   You cannot edit the document while in Print Preview.

To preview font variations, make sure you've selected WordPerfect Printer Drivers in the Select Printer dialog box; previewing with the Windows printer option in effect results in all fonts appearing the same, no matter which printer you choose.

See Also   Button Bar, Display, Printer Select

PRINTER SELECT

The Printer Select command displays a list of available printers for WordPerfect and Windows. Depending on the printer drivers you choose, you can select a number of printer configuration options.

To Select a Printer

1.   Choose File ➤ Select Printer.

2.   Select the set of printer drivers (WordPerfect or Windows) to use.

3. From the list of available printers, highlight the printer you want.

4. Choose **S**elect. The name of the selected printer appears on the status line of the Print dialog box.

To Add a Printer

You can add only WordPerfect printer drivers from within Word-Perfect. Make sure WordPerfect is selected in the Printer Driver box.

1. Choose **F**ile ➤ Select Printer.

2. Select **A**dd.

3. The Add Printer dialog box will apear, listing all of the printer (.ALL) files in the current directory path.

4. If the printer you want isn't listed, choose **C**hange. A Select Directory dialog box appears, which enables you to change drives and directories and search for your printer files.

5. When you find the printer file you want, select Add and the printer files will be listed in the Add Printer dialog box.

To list all .PRS files, select **P**rinter Files in the Add Printer dialog box. The change options can also be used for the .PRS files. A .PRS file is a driver for a printer you have already installed; WordPerfect maintains .ALL files for other printers you can install.

To Set Up a Printer

1. Choose **F**ile ➤ Select Printer.

2. Highlight the printer name and select S**e**tup.

3. Choose one or more of the editing options from the Setup dialog box.

Name of Printer: Enter a name of up to 36 characters for the printer definition. This name will be displayed on the Select Printer screen and is independent of the printer definition file name.

Path for Downloadable Fonts and Printer Commands: Enter the full path name or click on the File Select box to choose a path.

Current Initial Font: Shows the current intial font setting. You can choose a font type and point size from the list. A sample of the selected font is shown in the display screen.

Current Sheet Feeder: Shows the current setting and available options. Highlight the sheet feeder you want and choose Select. Remember, a single paper bin on a laser printer is *not* a sheet feeder.

Destination Port: Select the port for your printer: LPT1-LPT3, COM1-COM4, and File. When File is chosen, the Filename text box waits for you to enter a destination file name.

Network Printer: Click on this box to designate the printer as a network printer.

Cartridge/Fonts: Choose the cartridges and downloadable fonts you'll be using with the printer. The options in this feature depend on the type of printer files (.ALL) available (see the Cartridges and Fonts command reference).

4. Click OK to return to the Select Printer dialog box.

To Copy or Delete a Printer Definition

1. Choose File ➤ Select Printer.

2. Highlight the printer name you want to copy.

3. Choose Copy or Delete.

4. If you chose Copy, the Copy Printer dialog box appears. Click OK to copy the displayed file name or type in a new file name in the Printer Filename box. The copied file name will appear on the next line of the Select Printer list box.

5. If you chose Delete, the *Delete (printer name)* message will appear. To confirm the deletion, select Yes.

To reinstate a deleted printer definition, choose the Printer Files (.PRS) option in the Add Printers dialog box. Select the printer from the list and choose **Add**.

To View Information on a Printer

1. Choose File ➤ Select Printer.

2. Highlight the desired printer.

3. Click on Info and choose Printer or Sheet Feeder.

4. Click Close to return to the Select Printer dialog box.

To Update a Printer Definition

Update is used to update your .PRS files when a newer version of an .ALL file is obtained. It's best to rename or delete old .ALL files. Run Install to copy new .ALL files to your printer directory, and then use Update.

1. Choose File ➤ Select Printer.

2. Highlight the definition you want to update.

3. Choose Setup to define the printer options. Then choose OK.

4. Choose Update.

5. Select Close.

● **NOTES** The selected printer driver is used to print your document and display it on the Print Preview screen.

Basic printer information is stored in files with .ALL extensions in the printer files directory (see the Location of Files command reference). Adding or copying printer definitions extracts relevant printer information from .ALL files and stores it in files with .PRS extensions. Editing options update the .PRS files.

REDLINING AND STRIKEOUT

Redline and strikeout are often used to mark changes in contracts and other legal documents. Redline indicates text to be inserted; strikeout marks text to be deleted. You can choose to use the default redline method specific to your printer or choose to have redline characters appear in the margin.

To Insert Redline or Strikeout

1. Select the text to be redlined or struck over.
2. Choose Font ➤ Font (F9) and check the appropriate box in the Appearance area of the Font dialog box.
3. Choose OK.

To Change the Redlining Method for the Current Document

1. Choose Layout ➤ Document ➤ Redline Method (Ctrl+Shift+F9,R).
2. Choose a redline option (see Options).
3. Click OK.

To Change the Redlining Method for All New Documents

1. Choose File ➤ Preferences ➤ Print ➤ Redline Method.
2. Choose a redline option (see Options).
3. Click OK.

To Remove All Redline and Strikeover Marks

1. Choose **Tools** ➤ Do**c**ument Compare ➤ **R**emove
Markings to open the Remove Markings dialog box.

2. If you choose Leave Redline Markings, only Strikeout
characters are deleted.

3. Click OK.

● **OPTIONS**   Most printers mark redlined text with a shaded
background but you can change the marking with one of these redline options:

Printer Dependent	Mark text using instructions in the printer definition (.PRS) file. You cannot change the redline character when you choose this option.
Mar**k** Left Margin	Place redline characters along the left margin.
Mark **A**lternating Margins	Place redline characters along the left margin for even-numbered pages and along the right margin for odd-numbered pages.

For Left or Alternating redlining, you must indicate the redline
character to be used (the default is vertical bar " | ").

See Also   Document Compare, Font Attributes, Printer Select

REPLACE

The Replace command lets you search and replace characters and
WordPerfect codes within an entire document or a selected portion
of one.

To Replace Text

1. Position the insertion point where the replacement should begin.

2. Choose Edit ➤ Replace (Ctrl+F2) to open the Search and Replace dialog box.

3. In the Search For box, type the text you want to replaced.

4. In the Replace With box, type the text you want inserted in place of the search text. If you want only to remove the search text without replacing it, don't type any text.

5. If you want to search only the body of the main text (and not headers, footers, endnotes, etc.) choose Search Document Body Only.

6. In the Direction menu, choose Forward or Backward to search for text after the insertion point or before the insertion point.

7. Choose Search Next or Replace All. Search Next stops at the first occurrence of the search text string, then choose Replace to replace the text or Search Next to skip the text and go to the next occurrence. Replace All automatically replaces every occurrence of the search text.

To Replace Codes

1. Position the insertion point where the replacement should begin.

2. Select Edit ➤Replace (Ctrl+F2).

3. Position the insertion point in the Search For box.

4. Choose Codes to open the Codes dialog box.

5. Choose the code you want to search for and click on Insert. If you want to search for text between a pair of codes, choose the first code and click on Insert, type the search text, and then choose the second code and click Insert again.

6. Repeat steps 3 and 5 for the Replace With box.

7. Select Close to close the Codes dialog box.

● **NOTES** When specifying the search or replacement strings, you can click the Codes button to choose text formatting codes.

Search is not case sensitive unless you specify a capital letter. If the first letter of a word is capitalized, the first letter of the replacement word is also capitalized, even if you don't specify it.

You can use wildcards in the Search For box by choosing the Any Char option in place of a character. The wildcard cannot be the first character.

If you use Replace with selected text, the operation will be confined to that portion of your document.

See Also Codes, Search

RETRIEVE

The Retrieve command lets you bring a file into the current document. The retrieved document is added at the insertion point. This feature is similar to Open, except that Retrieve does not open a new window.

To Retrieve a File at the Insertion Point

1. Position the insertion point where you want the retrieved document inserted.

2. Choose File ➤ Retrieve to open the Retrieve File dialog box.

3. Enter the Filename to retrieve or select a name from the list and click Retrieve.

4. To insert the file into the current document, click Yes.

5. If prompted, enter the file's password and click OK.

● **NOTES** If the file you want is in another directory, you must type in the full path name in order to retrieve it.

WordPerfect 4.2 and 5.0 files are automatically converted into the Word-Perfect for Windows file format when they are retrieved. If you try to retrieve a non-WordPerfect file, the Convert File Format message box appears. Choose OK to convert the file. Use the Convert Program if you want to convert documents to WordPerfect format before retrieving them (see the Convert Program command reference).

To retrieve graphics, choose Figure from Graphics menu, then select the file name and choose Retrieve.

See Also   Convert Program, Exit, File Manager, Graphics and Graphic Boxes, Initial Codes, Open, Password, Save/Save As, Selecting Text

REVEAL CODES

WordPerfect uses codes to implement most formatting features. These codes are hidden unless you open the Reveal Codes window.

To Reveal Hidden Codes

1. Choose View ➤ Reveal Codes (Alt+F3). The Reveal Codes window appears in the lower half of your screen.

2. To close Reveal Codes, choose View ➤ Reveal Codes (Alt+F3).

● **NOTES**   The Reveal Codes window enables you to check for proper formatting, delete a code, or ensure that relevant codes are included when you select text (see the Selecting Text command reference).

If the formatting codes are not visible (including the text and cursor), experiment with the color settings in the Draft Mode Colors dialog box.

The Reveal Codes Window Figure 13 shows a screen with the Reveal Codes window open. The top section of the screen is the normal document window; the lower portion, which displays codes and text, is the Reveal Codes window.

The Reveal Codes cursor is usually displayed as a horizontal rectangle that highlights characters and codes as you move through the document window. The cursors on both screens are at exactly the same place in the document and both move together.

Codes are displayed in reverse video within square brackets to distinguish them from text. Some codes show more information when you place the Reveal Codes cursor directly on them.

There are two basic types of codes: unpaired codes, where a single code completely defines the feature (e.g., **[Comment]**); and paired codes, which have a start code to indicate where the formatting

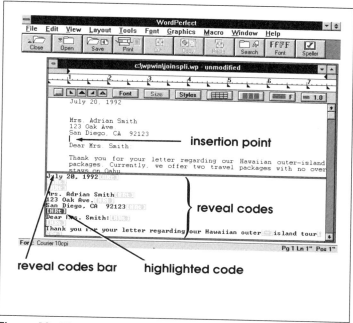

Figure 13: The Reveal Codes window

starts and an end code to indicate where it ends (e.g., **[Bold On]** and **[Bold Off]**). See Table 1 for a list of WordPerfect for Windows formatting codes.

To Delete a Formatting Code
Place the Reveal Codes cursor over the *code* for the feature, and then press the Delete (Del) key. This technique also deletes graphics, table and column definitions, and any other feature that inserts a code into your document (see the Delete Operations command reference). Deleting one code of a paired code deletes both codes. You can undelete unpaired codes, but not paired codes.

To Copy or Move a Formatting Code
It's often handy to be able to copy or move complex codes, like graphics boxes, that take some time to set up. To do this, turn Reveal Codes on, then select a block of text that contains paired codes (you cannot select the codes alone). Then open the Edit menu and select the relevant comands to cut, copy, paste, or append the selected codes.

See Also
Auto Code Placement, Codes, Delete Operations, Display, Move, Selecting Text, Undelete, Window

RULER

The ruler provides shortcuts for choosing fonts, styles, line spacing, and justification, and for creating and changing tables, columns, margins, and tab stops.

As illustrated in Figure 14, the ruler has three sections: the margins area on top, the tab stops in the middle, and a Button Bar on the bottom. (The Environment Settings dialog box lets you move the button bar to the top. The following procedures assume the default ruler settings.)

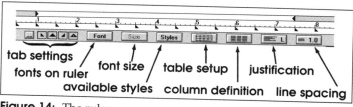

Figure 14: The ruler

To Turn the Ruler On/Off

To turn the ruler on or off:

- Choose **View ➤ R**uler (Alt+Shift+F3).

To Change the Margins with the Ruler

1. Move the insertion point to the location where you want to change the margins, or select text.

2. Move the mouse pointer to either the left or right margin icon at the top of the ruler.

3. Hold down the left mouse button and drag the icon to its new position.

To Change Tab Stops with the Ruler

1. Move the insertion point to the location where you want to change the tab stops, or select text.

2. Move the mouse pointer onto the tab stops section of the ruler.

- To move a tab stop, drag it to its new location.
- To delete a tab stop, drag it off the ruler.
- To add a tab stop, drag any one of the tab icons next to the Font button up into position in the tab stops section of the ruler. (If you want dot leaders at the tab stop, click the dot leaders button to the left of the tab icons before dragging the icon onto the ruler.)
- To get to the Tab Set dialog box, double-click any tab stop icon.

- To select multiple tab stops, position the mouse pointer between any existing icons, hold down the left mouse button, and drag the mouse pointer through the tab stops you want to select. After you release the mouse button, you can then drag the entire group to a new position, or drag them off the ruler.

To Choose Fonts with the Ruler

1. Position the insertion point to where you want to change the font, or select text.

2. Click and hold the Font button. Drag the highlight to the font you want to choose.

If you want to add more fonts to the ruler's Font button:

1. Double-click the Font button on the ruler (or press F9) to see the Font dialog box.

2. Choose Assign to Ruler. You'll see the Ruler Fonts Menu dialog box.

3. In the Font List, double-click any fonts that you want to add to the ruler, or highlight any font and choose Add.

4. Choose OK from the next two dialog boxes to return to the document window.

To remove a font from the ruler's Font button, double-click it in the Fonts on Ruler list box in step 3.

To Size Text with the Ruler

If the insertion point is currently in text that's displayed with a scalable font, you can change its point size from the ruler:

1. Position the insertion point to where you want to change the point size, or select the text to resize.

2. Click and hold the Size button on the Ruler. Drag the highlight to the option you want.

You can also double-click the Size button to get to the Font dialog box.

To Choose Styles with the Ruler

1. Move the insertion point to where you want to activate a
style, or select the text to which you want to assign a style.

2. Click the Styles button on the ruler, and drag the highlight
to the desired style.

You can also double-click the Styles button to get to the Styles
dialog box.

To Create a Table with the Ruler

1. Move the insertion point to the location where you want
to place the table.

2. Click on the tables icon button and hold the left mouse
button. You'll see a 10 × 10 grid, representing the columns
and rows in your table. Drag the highlight to select a table
size of up to 32 columns and 42 rows.

3. Release the mouse button and a blank table appears.

To Change Table
Column Widths with the Ruler

1. Move the insertion point anywhere within the table. The
current column positions appear as down-pointing
triangles in the margins area of the ruler.

2. Drag any column icon to set the new width for the column.

Columns to the right of the current column will automatically be resized to accommodate the change. You can change the width of the entire table by dragging the margin icons at the far left and right edges of the ruler. If you hold down the Shift key while dragging the column marker, you move only that marker. If you hold down the Ctrl key, the columns to the right move but keep their original width.

To Create Columns with the Ruler

To create newspaper-style columns with the ruler:

1. Move the insertion point to where you want to activate columns or select text.

2. Click and hold the columns icon button. Drag the highlight to the number of columns you want to create.

You can also move the insertion point to wherever you want to deactivate columns, and then choose Columns Off.

To Change Column Widths with the Ruler

1. Move the insertion point to anywhere within the existing columns. Icons in the margins area of the ruler indicate the current column positions; grayed areas indicate gutters (space between columns).

2. Drag any column position icon to a new position.

To Change Justification with the Ruler

1. Move the insertion point to the location where you want to change the justification.

2. Click and hold the justification icon button. Drag the highlight to the new setting: Left, Right, Center, or Full.

To Change Line Spacing with the Ruler

1. Move the insertion point to the location where you want to change line spacing.

2. Click and hold the line spacing icon button. Drag the highlight to the new setting.

To Change Default Ruler Settings

1. Choose File ➤ Preferences ➤ Environment (Ctrl+ Shift+F1, E).

2. Choose any combination of the following ruler options:

Tabs Snap to Ruler Grid: When enabled, tab stops along the ruler automatically snap to invisible grid lines spaced every 1/16 inch across the document.

Show Ruler Guides: When enabled, a dotted line appears down the document window while dragging tab stops or margin icons on the ruler, so you can see how text will align on the page.

Ruler Buttons on Top: When enabled, moves the Button Bar to the top of the ruler.

Automatic Ruler Display: When enabled, the ruler appears automatically every time you open a new document window.

3. Choose OK to leave the dialog box.

● **NOTES**   In Draft mode, text in the document window may not accurately reflect tab stops and margins along the ruler.

When Auto Code Placement is on, tab, column, justification, and line spacing codes are automatically placed at the beginning of the current paragraph.

See Also   Auto Code, Columns, Draft Mode, Environment, Font, Justification, Margins, Tab

SAVE/SAVE AS

To Save a Document

1.   Choose File ➤ Save (Shift+F3).

2.   If the file has previously been saved, WordPerfect automatically saves the file under the previous name. If not, the Save As dialog box will appear (see below).

To Save a Document under a New Name

1.   Choose File ➤ Save As (F3).

2.   In the Document to be saved box, enter the file name or full path name for the document, or choose **S**ave or press ↵ to accept the displayed name.

3.   If the file name already exists on disk, WordPerfect will display a message asking you if you want to replace the existing file. Choose **Y**es to replace it, or **N**o or ↵ to return to step 2.

To Save a File in a Non-WordPerfect Format

1.   Choose File ➤ Save As (F3).

2.   Enter the file name in the "Document to be saved" box.

3.   Choose a file format by clicking on the arrow icon to the right side of the Format box, scrolling through the list, and clicking to highlight the desired format. If the specific program is not listed, choose one of the following:

ASCII Text (DOS) preserves only the text, without formatting codes, for use in non-Windows applications.

ANSI Text (Windows) preserves only the text, without formatting codes, for use in Windows applications.

ASCII Generic Word Processor (DOS) saves the document in a generic word processing format, without

WordPerfect-specific codes but with tabs, hard returns, and indentation, for use with non-Windows applications.

ANSI Generic Word Processor (Windows) saves the file in the same format as ASCII Generic Word Processor (DOS) but for use in Windows applications.

ASCII Delimited Text (DOS) preserves the text without formatting codes and inserts field and record delimiters for use with non-Windows database and spreadsheet applications.

ANSI Delimited Text (Windows) preserves the text without formatting and inserts field and record delimiters for use with Windows spreadsheet and database applications.

The **WP5.0** or **WP4.2** formats save a document for use in WordPerfect 5.0 or 4.2, respectively.

4. Click **Save**.

To Close a Document Window

1. Choose File ➤ Close (Ctrl+F4).

2. If the document is new or has been modified since it was last saved, WordPerfect will ask if you want to save the changes to the document. Choose **Yes** to save the changes, **No** to discard changes, or **Cancel** or ↵ to return to the document.

● **NOTES** The Save command saves your document to a file on disk and returns you to the document window. The Save As command saves a file under a new name or in non-WordPerfect format and returns to the document window. Both commands close the document.

The Exit command (Alt+F4) also enables you to save a document, but it clears the screen after saving the file.

Unless you turn off the Fast Save option in the Environment menu, WordPerfect saves your document without print formatting. This feature can speed up save operations but will slow down printing, as the print formatting must be done at that time.

You can password protect files by selecting Password (see the Password command reference).

See the Master Document command reference for details on saving master documents and subdocuments.

File Naming Rules   File names can have up to eight characters, plus an optional period and a one- to three-letter extension. Full path names include a drive letter, the name of each directory above the file separated by backslashes (\), and the file name.

Never use spaces in path names, file names, or extensions, and avoid using extensions with special meanings to DOS or Word-Perfect (such as .COM or .EXE).

Unless you enter a full path name, the file is saved in your default directory.

Sample file names are: MEMO   MEMO.EAO   MYSTUFF.1

Sample path names are: D:\MEMOS\MYSTUFF.1 A:MEMO.EAO

See Also   Backup, Document Summary, Environment, Exit, File Manager, Master Document, Password, Retrieve

SEARCH

The Search command is useful for quickly moving to a certain place in your document or to extend a block of selected text. You can search through your text for a specific combination of characters and codes.

To Search for Text and Codes

1.   Move the insertion point to the location where the search should begin.

2.   Choose **Edit** ➤ Search (F2).

3. Enter the string to search for. The string may include characters, formatting codes, or both.

4. Select the Direction to search (default is forward).

5. Select Search Document Body Only if you want to search only the main document body, skipping headers, footers, endnotes, footnotes, graphic box captions, and text boxes. The default searches the entire document.

6. Select Search.

To Specify a Code to Search

You can search for single or paired codes, or a combination of codes and text, by inserting the codes in the Search For text box:

1. Click the Codes button in the Search dialog box.

2. Scroll the pop-up list to the desired code and click to highlight it.

3. Choose Insert to add the code to the search string in the Search For text box.

4. Repeat steps 2–3 as necessary.

5. Choose Close to return to the Search dialog box.

You can also search for patterns by selecting Any Char from the Codes list. For example, [Bold On][Any Char][Bold Off] will search for any single character that is flanked by bold codes. To search for merge codes, check the Merge Codes box to display a list of merge codes.

To Continue a Search

You may search again for the same pattern in either direction.

- To find the next occurrence of the last pattern you sought, choose Edit ➤ Search Next (Shift+F2).

- To find the previous occurrence of the last pattern you searched, choose Edit ➤ Search Previous (Alt+F2).

• **NOTES**   You can use the Viewer in the File Manager to search through an unopened file. If you use the Viewer, the search yields all the names of files that contain the word or string you are searching for.

If you want to search for a string or code and replace it with another, see the Replace command reference.

Entering the Search String   Enter a search string by typing the text you want to find. Lowercase letters match both lowercase and uppercase letters, while uppercase letters match uppercase letters only. To find a specific word (like "the") within a sentence, press the spacebar before and after the word. Otherwise, search will find all occurrences of the string, including those within a word, such as "their" or "other."

When repeating a search, you can edit the search string as necessary by selecting Search again and editing the string in the Search For box. Then click Search.

See Also   Codes, File Manager, Replace

SELECTING TEXT

Selecting text lets you identify text to be moved, copied or deleted, and also lets you activate print attributes (bold, italic), styles, and other features *after* you've already typed the text.

To Select Text with the Mouse

1. Position the I beam at one end of the block.

2. Hold down the left mouse button and drag the mouse pointer to the other end of the block. The text will be highlighted.

3. Release the left mouse button.

You can also:

- Double-click to select the current word.
- Triple-click to select the current sentence.
- Quadruple-click to select the current paragraph.

To Select Text with the Keyboard

1. Position the I beam at one end of the block.

2. Choose Edit ➤ Select. Choose the item from the menu that you wish to select, and press ↵. Or, hold down the Shift key and use the arrow, Page Up, Page Down, Home, or End keys to extend the selection. In either case, the selected text will be highlighted.

3. You can also use Search (F2) to extend the selection to a specific character, word, code, or phrase.

● **NOTES** You can also use Shift+Ctrl or Shift+Alt together with a direction key to select a specific portion of text. See the Keystrokes (Shift+Alt) and Keystrokes (Shift+Ctrl) entries in WordPerfect Help for a listing of these keys.

You can select text, and then perform the operations listed in Table 12 on that selected text.

Table 12: Operations you can perform after selecting

Operation on Selected Text	Keystrokes	See Also
Boldface, italics, underline, etc.	Select Font, then choose the desired text attribute	Font Attributes
Center	Select Layout ➤ Line ➤ Center (Shift+F7)	Center

Table 12: Operations you can perform after selecting (continued)

Operation on Selected Text	Keystrokes	See Also
Change the size or appearance	Select Font ➤ Font, then choose Appearance or Size	Font Attributes
Convert to upper or lowercase	Select Edit ➤ Convert Case, then choose Uppercase or Lowercase	Case Conversion
Convert to a comment	Select Tools ➤ Comment ➤ Create	Document Comments
Convert to a table	Select Layout ➤ Tables ➤ Create (Ctrl-F9,C), then select other table options	Tables
Copy (enhanced keyboards)	Press Ctrl+Ins, then move cursor and press Shift+Ins	Retrieve
Delete	Press Del or Backspace	Delete Operations
Flush Right	Select Layout ➤ Justification ➤ Right (Ctrl+R) or Layout ➤ Line ➤ Flush Right (Alt+F7)	Flush Right
Format with a style	Select Layout ➤ Styles, then select style options	Styles

Table 12: Operations you can perform after selecting (continued)

Operation on Selected Text	Keystrokes	See Also
Mark for Reference	Select **Tools ➤ Mark** Text (F12), then select an option	Cross-Reference, Index, Lists, Table of Authorities, Table of Contents
Move (enhanced keyboards)	Shift+Del, then move the cursor and press Shift+Ins	Move, Retrieve
Move, copy, delete, or append	Select **Edit**, then choose **Cut**, **Copy**, **Paste**, or **Append**	Move
Print	Select **File ➤ Print ➤ Print** (F5,P)	Print
Protect from Page/Column Breaks	Select **Layout ➤ Page ➤ B**lock Protect (Alt+F9,B)	Page Breaks
Save as separate file	Select **File ➤ Save**, then enter the file name	Retrieve
Sort	Select **Tools ➤ Sort** (Ctrl+Shift+ F12), then select sort options	Sorting and Selecting
Spell check	Select **Tools ➤ S**peller (Ctrl+F1), then set speller options	Speller
Word Count	Select **Tools ➤ Word** Count	

If you type a character while a block is selected, the entire block will be replaced with that character.

To "unselect" selected text without performing an operation, move the insertion point or click the left mouse button.

Before selecting text that contains codes, you may wish to turn on Reveal Codes (View ➤ Reveal Codes or Alt+F3) to ensure that codes are properly included, or excluded, from the selection.

See Also   Tables

SHORTCUT KEYS

You can often use combinations from the keyboard to accomplish a common task quickly.

To Set Your Own Shortcut Keys

1. Choose File ➤ Preferences ➤ Keyboard and click the Create button.

2. Using the Item Types list, choose the type of item you want to assign a shortcut key to.

3. Select the item to assign the shortcut key to.

4. Enter the key combination you want to use.

5. Click the Assign button.

6. Repeat steps 3–5 for each shortcut key.

7. Select Save As. The Save Keyboard File dialog box appears. Type in the file name and select Save.

8. Click OK.

● **NOTES**   If you are using a keyboard definition other than the default, you can change the assignment of any of its keys using the steps above.

From the Keyboard Editor dialog box, you can **U**nassign shortcut keys. This frees up shortcut keys for use with other commands.

The Home Key   If you are used to the way the Home key worked in previous versions of WordPerfect, you can reset it to operate in the same way in WordPerfect for Windows. In the Keyboard Edit dialog box, select the Home Key **W**orks Like DOS WP 5.1 check box. You can make this change only in a Keyboard definition you have created or edited; you cannot edit the CUA keyboard.

SORTING AND SELECTING

These procedures sort and extract records and selected text in a document. They are particularly useful for alphabetizing bibliographies, name lists, and tables.

To Sort and Extract a List

1. Select the text you want to sort (if you don't want to sort the whole document), or position the insertion point anywhere inside a table.

2. Choose **T**ools ➤ Sort (Ctrl+Shift+F12).

3. Choose a record type (see Records and Fields).

4. Choose the sort order: **A**scending or **D**escending.

5. Add any additional key definitions to the list (see Options).

6. If extracting records, enter the **R**ecord Selection criteria (see Options).

7. Click OK and press ⏎ to begin the sort.

● **RECORDS AND FIELDS**   *Records* are the lines, paragraphs, or text blocks to be sorted. Each record can contain sort keys consisting of *cells, fields, lines,* and *words.*

Fields are separated by tabs or indents in lines or paragraphs, and by {END FIELD} codes in merge records. In tables, each cell is a field. Records can contain many fields. Each corresponding field should contain the same type of information.

Lines are separated by hard or soft returns.

Words are separated by spaces, forward slashes (/), or hard hyphens (Ctrl+–) within a line or field. To select multiple words for sorting as if they were single words, place a hard space (Ctrl+spacebar) between the words.

Record types are:

Merge Record (secondary merge file)	Records are separated by {END RECORD} codes. Sort keys are divided into Fields, Lines, and Words.
Line	Each line is a record. Sort keys are divided into Fields and Words.
Paragraph	Each paragraph is a record. Paragraphs must end with at least two hard returns [HRt]. Sort keys are divided into Lines, Fields, and Words.
Table Row	Each row is a record. Sort keys are divided into Cells (columns of text), Lines, and Words.

● **OPTIONS**   Select Record Type before choosing one or more of these options:

Record Type	Choose **L**ine, **P**aragraph, **M**erge Record, or **T**able Row for the record type. This option must be chosen before any other option.
Sort Order	Choose **A**scending (A-Z, 0–9, negative to positive), **D**escending (Z to A, 9–0, positive to negative), or **N**o Sort (extract without sorting).

Key Definitions

Lets you define up to nine sort keys. Key1 has first priority, key2 has second priority, etc. Define the key *Type* as **A**lpha (letters) or **N**umeric (numbers, dollar signs, commas, and periods). Then indicate the *Field, Line, Word,* or *Cell* numbers within the key. Use positive numbers to number from left to right or top to bottom, or negative numbers to number from right to left or bottom to top. Additional keys are only used when the higher-ordered key portion of two records are identical. Use the **I**nsert key and **D**elete key buttons to add or remove keys.

Record Selection

A **R**ecord Selection description is used to indicate which records should be sorted and extracted. *Important:* Records within the text selection that do not meet the Record Selection criteria will be deleted!

Specify keys as "key" followed by a number (e.g., key1). Values can be numbers and/or letters. Use keyg instead of a key number for a global selection where any field can qualify (e.g., keyg=Bermuda will match "Bermuda" in any field).

Key statements may be combined, such as Key1>=Jones * Key1<=Smith, where the * denotes a logical AND. Selection is done from left to right unless you use parentheses for grouping, as in key5=male * (key1=Smith + key1=Jones).

Table 13 shows the available logical operators and sample key statements.

● **NOTES**   For safety, back up your input file or on-screen document first.

By default, records are sorted alphabetically according to the first word in the record. Numbers are sorted negative to positive if you select Ascending order. The rules are reversed for Descending order. Use No Sort to extract records without sorting them.

Table 13: Logical operators used in selections

Operator	Description	Sample
+	"OR": selects records that meet the conditions of either key	key1=Smith + key3>CA
*	"AND": selects records that meet the conditions of both keys	key1=Smith * key3=CA
=	Selects records that match a specific value	key3=CA
<>	Selects records that do not match a specific value	key3<>CA
>	Selects records that are greater than a specific value	key4>92123
<	Selects records that are less than a specific value	key4<92123
>=	Selects records that are greater than or equal to a specific value	key4>=92123
<=	Selected records are less than or equal to a specific value	key4<=92123

Codes within a record will be sorted along with the record, possibly affecting the results of paired codes.

● **EXAMPLE**   Figure 15 shows a sample list of names and addresses, with each column of text separated by a tab stop. The Sort

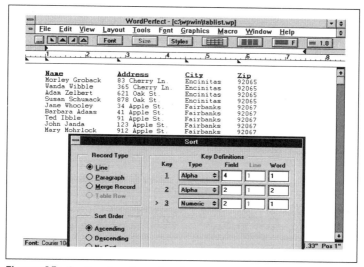

Figure 15: Sorting by zip code, street name, street number

dialog box shows the sort keys defined to sort the list by zip code (Field 4, Word 1), by street name within each zip code (Field 3, Word 2), and by street number within each street (Field 3, Word 1).

See Also   Language, Merge Operations, Tables

SPACES (HARD AND SOFT)

You can insert hard or soft spaces between words. Use hard spaces to have more than one word treated as a single word for formatting, hyphenation, and sorting purposes. Use soft spaces to treat each word separately.

To Insert a Soft or Hard Space

- For a soft space, simply press the spacebar.

- For a hard space, select **Layout** ➤ Line (Shift+F9), and then choose Special Codes. Select Hard Space[HdSpc] and click **Insert**.

● **NOTES** Hard spaces are especially helpful for keeping dates or names together on a line.

Hard spaces insert a code ([   ]) into your document; soft spaces do not insert codes.

See Also Hyphenation, Sorting and Selecting

SPECIAL CHARACTERS

The Special Characters command enables you to insert characters such as bullets and foreign letters that are not available from your keyboard.

To Insert Special Characters

1. Position the insertion point where you want the character.

2. Choose **Font** ➤ WP Characters (Ctrl+W).

3. In the WordPerfect Characters dialog box, the ASCII character set is displayed by default. If you don't see the character you need, use the Set list button or the arrow keys to select another character set.

4. Click on the character you want or enter its number in the Number text box. This box shows the set number and then the character number, separated by a comma. Numbering starts at 0, not 1 (except for the ASCII set, whose first 32 "characters" are nonprinting).

5. Choose Insert. To insert additional characters, repeat steps 3 and 4 above, then choose Close. Otherwise, choose Insert and Close.

See Also Equations, Overstrike

SPELLER

The Speller checks for spelling errors, double words, words containing numbers, and capitalization errors, and can be used to suggest words that fit a pattern. You can also look up words by phonetic spelling and display a list of words that match a specified pattern.

To Start a Spelling Check

1. Optionally, move the insertion point to the word or page you want to check, or select a block of text.

2. Choose Tools ➤ Speller (Ctrl+F1).

3. Click the Check button and select the scope of the spell check:

Word	Checks the word the insertion point is on or immediately following the insertion point
Page	Checks the page the insertion point is on
Selected Text	Checks the currently selected text
Document	Checks the entire document
To End of Document	Checks from the insertion point to the end of the document
To End of Page	Checks from the insertion point to the end of the page
To End of Selection	Checks from the insertion point to the end of the selection

4. Click Start to begin.

To Set Speller Options

The Options menu enables you to set the parameters for the spell checking of text.

- Words with Numbers: Disabling this option will instruct the Speller to skip any words that contain numeric values, such as *386SX*.

- Duplicate Words: Disabling this option will instruct the Speller to skip identical words which appear consecutively.

- Irregular Capitalization: Disabling this option will instruct the Speller to ignore words with nonstandard capitalization, such as dBASE.

- Move to Bottom: This option moves the Speller window to the far bottom of the screen and centers it.

All options are enabled as the default.

To Make Spelling Corrections

When the Speller is started, it will highlight any word that it cannot find in the main or supplemental dictionaries. The Suggestions window will show possible replacements for the misspelled word. You can then either:

- Select the correct word in the suggestions box and click Replace or press ↵ to replace the misspelled word with the suggested word.

- Select Add to add the word to the supplemental dictionary.

- Select Skip Once to skip this occurrence of the word.

- Select Skip Always to skip all occurrences of the word.

- Edit the word in the Word text box and click Replace or press ↵ to replace the misspelled word with the edited version.

If a duplicate word is discovered, you may Disable further checking for duplicate words, delete the 2nd word, or ignore this duplication and Continue.

If a word with irregular case is discovered, you may **D**isable further case checking, **C**ontinue, or **R**eplace the word with regular case. Replace uses the first three characters of the word to determine proper capitalization. For example, *THis* becomes *This*; *tHIs* becomes *THIs*; *thIs* becomes *this*; and *iS* becomes *Is* (in two-letter words only).

To Suggest a Spelling

The Speller can suggest words based on a character pattern.

1. Choose **T**ools ➤ **S**peller (Ctrl+F1).

2. Enter a word pattern in the **W**ord text box.

3. Choose **S**uggest. Suggested spellings for the word appear in the Suggestions box.

A word pattern is composed of characters and "wildcards." Use a question mark (?) to represent a single character, and an asterisk (*) to represent multiple characters. For example, *chil?* results in *child*, *Chile*, *chili*, and *chill*, while **kmarks* retrieves *bookmarks* and *pockmarks*.

To Change Speller Dictionaries

WordPerfect uses a built-in main dictionary (WP{WP}US.LEX), a built-in supplementary dictionary (WP{WP}US.SUP), and (optionally) your own supplementary dictionary for spell checking and hyphenation.

To change the main or supplemental dictionaries:

• Choose **D**ictionary from the Speller dialog box and select the name of the dictionary you want.

The Add option adds new words to the supplementary dictionary during spell checking. You can also edit dictionaries using the Speller Utility program (SPELL.EXE) or WordPerfect itself (for supplementary dictionaries only).

To create a personal supplementary dictionary using WordPerfect, clear the screen and enter a list of words, one word per line. You can include dashes (–) to indicate where words should be hyphenated. Sort the list (see the Sorting and Selecting command reference) and store your dictionary in the directory listed in Location of Files (File ➤ Preferences ➤ Location of Files) for supplementary dictionaries. WordPerfect automatically supplies the .SUP extension.

● **NOTES** Turning the Suggestions option off will make spell checking somewhat faster, but removes the advantage of being able to select the correct word.

The Edit pull-down menu lets you use the Clipboard and the Speller together. You can Cut, Copy, or Paste between the Clipboard and the Word text box. The Undo option cancels your most recent edit of the word.

The Match pull-down menu offers an alternative way of entering wildcards in Speller search patterns. Your options are 1character and Multiple Characters.

The Speller Utility is a character-based (i.e., non-Windows) editing application that is also included with WordPerfect 5.1 for DOS. You can use it to display the word list, add or delete words, or find a word in the WordPerfect dictionary. To run it, begin at the File Manager (File ➤ File Manager ➤ File ➤ Run). Type **spell.exe** (specify a path if you've installed the utility somewhere other than the C:\WPWIN directory) and choose **R**un to start the utility.

See Also Hyphenation, Location of Files

SPREADSHEET LINK

These procedures enable you to copy information from a spreadsheet file and update the "linked" information in your WordPerfect document automatically whenever it changes in the spreadsheet. You can link WordPerfect to PlanPerfect (versions 3.0 through 5.1), Lotus 1-2-3 (versions 1.0 through 3.1), Microsoft Excel (version 3.0), Quattro, and Quattro Pro spreadsheets. Use the DDE Link feature to link a document to other Windows applications.

To Create a Spreadsheet Link

Before you can copy information from a spreadsheet file, you must create a link:

1. Position the insertion point where the spreadsheet information is to appear.

2. Choose Tools ➤ Spreadsheet ➤ Create Link.

3. Enter a spreadsheet file name or click the list button and select a name from the file list.

4. Enter the range of cells to be copied or select the range name (see Notes).

5. Choose Table (to link the data into a WordPerfect table) or Text.

6. Choose OK.

To Edit an Existing Spreadsheet Link

1. Position the insertion point inside the link you want to edit (between the [Link] and [End Link] codes).

2. Choose Tools ➤ Spreadsheet ➤ Edit Link.

3. Edit the link information in the dialog box.

4. Choose OK.

To Import Spreadsheet Data

You can acquire spreadsheet data without setting up links that automatically update the information. This is useful for a one-time data transfer.

1. Position the insertion point where the data is to appear.

2. Choose Tools ➤ Spreadsheet ➤ Import.

3. Enter the spreadsheet file name, range, and type (Table or Text) as above.

4. Choose OK.

● **NOTES**   A spreadsheet range is a rectangular section of the spreadsheet file, defined by naming the upper-left cell and the lower-right cell. Type the two numbers separated by a colon, a period, or two periods (e.g., A1:F35, A1.F35, or A1..F35). If you have named ranges in the spreadsheet file, the names will appear in the list box and you can select the name instead of typing the cell numbers.

If you link or import spreadsheet data as text, the cells are separated into columns by tabs and into rows by hard returns.

You can update all links in your WordPerfect file by choosing **Tools** ➤ Spreadsheet ➤ Update All Links. Choose Yes or No in the dialog box.

You also have the options of showing the link codes and of updating the links when you retrieve the file. Choose **Tools** ➤ Spreadsheet ➤ Link Options and click the check boxes for desired options.

See Also   DDE Link, Tables

STYLES

Styles are combinations of formatting commands that you can apply to individual words, lines, sentences, paragraphs, or even entire documents. Styles let you apply consistent formatting to your text.

To Create a Style

1.   Choose **Layout** ➤ Styles ➤ Create (Alt+F8,C).

2.   Enter a new style **Name** and **Description**.

3.   Select options from the **Type** and the **Enter Key Inserts** pop-up menus (see Editing Options).

4.   Choose OK.

5.   Enter the codes that define the style in the Style Editor window (see Notes).

6.   Click Close.

To Edit or Delete a Style

1. Choose Layout ➤ Styles (Alt+F8).

2. Highlight the style you want to edit or delete.

3. Choose Edit or Delete.

4. If you chose Edit, edit the text or codes in the Style Editor window and then click Close.

5. If you chose Delete, the Delete Style dialog box appears. Select a delete option: **Leave Format Codes**, **Delete Format Codes**, and Delete Definition **O**nly (see Style Options). Click OK.

6. Click Close.

To Apply a Style

1. Position the insertion point where the style should begin, or select a block of text.

2. Choose Layout ➤ Styles (Alt+F8), or select the Styles menu from the ruler.

3. Highlight the style you want. If you're using the ruler, the style will be applied.

4. If you're not using the ruler, choose **O**n.

● OPTIONS

Style Options

On   Turns on the highlighted style.

Off   Turns off the highlighted style (for paired styles only). You can also turn paired styles off by moving past the [Style Off] code (press →) or by pressing ↵ (if the Enter Key Inserts setting is set to Style **O**ff or Style **O**ff/On). Applying a paired style to *selected* text automatically inserts the [Style Off] code.

Create Lets you create a style.

Edit Lets you change the highlighted style.

Delete Deletes the highlighted style from the list. Leave Format Codes deletes the [Style On] and [Style Off] codes and leaves the formatting codes contained within the style in the document. Delete Format Codes removes all the associated codes from the document. Delete Definition Only deletes the formatting codes and retains the [Style On] and [Style Off] codes in the document.

Save As Saves the style list in a separate library file. Select this if you want to use the style list for documents other than the one you are currently editing. Enter a file name to store the list in the default style directory, or enter a full path name.

Retrieve Retrieves a style library file. Enter a file name or full path name, or use the File Manager. If the styles being retrieved have the same names as the existing styles, choose Yes to replace the existing styles, or No to retrieve only styles with different names. Retrieve options include Delete, Copy, Rename, and Find.

Editing Options

Name Enter up to 20 characters (including spaces) for the Style name.

Description Enter up to 54 characters (including spaces) for the Style definition (optional).

Type Choose Paired or Open. You can convert existing styles from one type to another.

Enter Key Inserts Determines what happens when ↵ is pressed. Select Hard Return if you want ↵ to insert a [HRt] code. Select Style Off to automatically turn off the style. Select Style Off/On to enable the ↵ key to alternately turn styles off and on.

● **NOTES**   *Open styles,* useful for formats that affect an entire document, only need to be turned on. *Paired styles* must be turned on [Style On] and off [Style Off]. *Outline styles,* used with outlines and paragraph numbering, can be open or paired.

Changes made to a style are instantly reflected everywhere you used that style in the document.

Style lists in subdocuments are combined into the master document; any subdocuments saved when you condense the master document will also contain the combined list of styles.

Entering Style Codes   After clicking OK in the Styles Properties window when creating a new style, control is passed to the Style Editor window. Choose the desired formatting features and enter text as usual. For paired styles, WordPerfect displays the following message in the Style editor:

> **Codes placed above this comment take effect when the style is turned on.**
> **Codes placed below this comment take effect when the style is turned off.**

Enter the codes that turn the style on before the comment, and the codes that turn it off after the comment. Click Close when done.

See Also   Codes, File Manager, Location of Files, Master Documents, Outline, Paragraph Numbering

TABLE OF AUTHORITIES

A Table of Authorities is used primarily in legal briefs to list where citations of specific cases and statutes occur throughout a document. You can divide it into sections according to the type of citation (e.g. federal or state statutes). Citations within each section are sorted alphanumerically.

Use the Table of Authorities (ToA) features to mark each citation in a Table of Authorities, define the ToA location and format, and generate a ToA.

The first occurrence of a citation in the document or subdocument is called the *full form*. After defining the full form, you can mark subsequent references to the same authority using the *short form*.

To Mark a Full Form Citation

1. Select the text you want to cite.

2. Choose Tools ➤ Mark Text ➤ ToA Full Form (F12,F).

3. Enter the section number (1–16) for the entry.

4. WordPerfect displays the full text of the citation in the Short Form text box. Edit the short form text to be used in subsequent citations. Click OK when done.

5. Edit the Full Form text, if necessary, and click Close.

To Mark a Short Form Citation

After you've marked the full form for the first occurrence of a citation, mark subsequent occurrences with a short form. The Search feature guarantees that you will find all subsequent citations.

1. Move the insertion point to the top of the document (press Ctrl+Home).

2. Choose Edit ➤ Search (or press F2).

3. Type the short form (or part of the short form).

4. Choose Search to start the search.

5. If the insertion point lands to the right of a valid short form citation, choose Tools ➤ Mark Text ➤ ToA Short Form (or press F12,S). If the text is not a citation, press Shift+F2 to find the next occurrence of the search string.

6. Press ↵ to accept the suggested short form citation, or enter the correct short form citation and then press ↵.

7. Repeat steps 2–6 for each remaining short form citation in the document.

To Define ToA Location and Section Format

1. Position the insertion point where you want the section to appear.

2. Choose Layout ➤ Page ➤ Page Break (Ctrl+↵) to start the table on a new page.

3. Enter a section heading and press ↵ as needed for blank lines.

4. Choose Tools ➤ Define ➤ Table of Authorities (Shift+F12, A).

5. Enter the section number (1–16).

6. Choose one or more ToA formatting options (see Options).

7. Click OK.

8. Optionally, insert a hard page break, as in step 2.

9. Optionally, choose Layout ➤ Page ➤ Numbering ➤ New Page Number and enter the original number of the page immediately following the ToA section. Then, choose Insert Page Number.

To Define Default Section Formats

1. Choose File ➤ Preferences ➤ Table of Authorities.

2. Choose the desired ToA formatting options (see Options).

3. Click OK.

To Edit the Full Form of a Citation

1. Choose View ➤ Reveal Codes (Alt+F3).

2. Position the insertion point to the immediate right of the [ToA...Full Form] code.

3. Choose Tools ➤ Mark Text ➤ ToA Edit Full Form (F12,E).

4. Edit the text of the full form. Click Close when done or Edit Short Form if you need to change the short form or give the citation a different section number.

5. Generate the Table (Tools ➤ Generate ➤ Yes) to see your changes.

To Generate a ToA

- Choose Tools ➤ Generate ➤ Yes (Alt+F12,Y).

● OPTIONS

Dot Leaders	Leave the box checked to have dot leaders precede flush right page numbers, or uncheck the box to omit dot leaders.
Underlining Allowed	Check the box to include existing underline codes in the text of the citation, or leave unchecked to omit them.
Blank Line Between Authorities	Leave the box checked to double-space the authorities, or turn off to single-space them.

● NOTES You can create a table of authorities for an individual document or for a master document. Place the ToA definition in the master document, *not* in a subdocument. Use Search (F2) to quickly position the insertion point during marking.

To delete a citation entry, choose View ➤ Reveal Codes (Alt+F3) and delete the appropriate [ToA] code.

See Also Generate, Page Numbering, Search, Selecting Text

TABLE OF CONTENTS

You can create a Table of Contents (ToC) for an individual document or for a master document.

Use the Table of Contents features to mark table of contents entries, define Table of Contents location and numbering style for each level, and generate a ToC.

To Mark Table of Contents Entries

1. Select the text and codes you want to include in the table of contents.

2. Choose **Tools** ➤ Mark Text ➤ Table of Contents (F12,C).

3. Enter the level number (1–5) for the entry, and click OK.

To Define the ToC
Location and Page Number Style

1. Position the insertion point where you want the ToC to appear (usually at the beginning of the document).

2. Enter a heading and press ↵ as needed to add blank lines.

3. Choose **Tools** ➤ Define ➤ Table of Contents (Shift+F12,C).

4. Choose one or more ToC formatting options (see Options).

5. Click OK.

6. Choose **Layout** ➤ Page ➤ Page Break (Ctrl+↵) to insert a hard page break.

7. Choose **Layout** ➤ Page ➤ Numbering ➤ New Page Number (Alt+F9,NN) and enter a number for the page immediately following the ToC. Then select Insert Page Number.

To Generate a ToC

• Choose **Tools** ➤ Generate ➤ Yes (Alt+F12,Y).

• OPTIONS

Number of Levels
Type a number (1–5) for the number of levels to include in the ToC. Each level will be indented one tab stop from the previous level.

Numbering Format	Choose a style for each level: **No** Numbering (no page numbers); Text **#** (page numbers follow entries and are preceded by a space); **Text** (#) Follows (page numbers are in parentheses one space following the entry); **Text #** (page numbers are flush right); or Text......# (dot leaders precede flush right page numbers).
Last Level in Wrapped Format	Check the box to wrap the last level flush left (if there is more than 1 level), or leave the box unchecked to prevent wrapping.

Place the ToC definition in the master document, *not* in a subdocument.

Although you can place your ToC anywhere in the document, it's best to put it at the beginning.

To delete a ToC entry, choose View ➤ Reveal Codes (Alt+F3) and delete the appropriate [Mark:ToC] or [End Mark:Toc] code.

See Also   Generate, Page Numbering, Selecting Text, Tabs

TABLES

Tables provide a convenient way to present and calculate information in rows and columns.

To Create a Table

1.   Position the insertion point where you want the table.

2.   Choose Layout ➤ Tables ➤ Create (Ctrl+F9,C).

3.   Enter the number of Columns.

4.   Enter the number of Rows.

5.   Click OK.

To Create a Table from Existing Text

Typically, any text you convert to a table will already be in a colum-nar format (parallel or newspaper). Make sure that only one [Tab] or [Insert] code separates each column of text. Then follow these steps to convert the text to a table:

1. Select the text.

2. Choose **L**ayout ➤ **T**ables ➤ **C**reate (Ctrl+F9,C).

3. Choose **T**abular Column or **P**arallel Column dpending on the structure of the text.

4. Click OK.

To Delete a Table

You can delete an entire table, its contents only, or its structure only.

1. Select all the cells in the table.

2. Press the Delete or Backspace key.

3. Choose **E**ntire Table, **C**ontents (text only), or **T**able Struc-ture (leave text) in the Delete Table dialog box.

4. Choose OK.

You can also delete a table by dragging the mouse over the entire table and pressing the Delete key.

To Select Table Elements for Editing

Tables have vertical *columns* and horizontal *rows* that intersect to form *cells*. Columns are labeled alphabetically from left to right, while rows are labeled numerically from top to bottom. Thus, A1 is the first cell, B1 is just to the right of A1, and A2 is just below A1.

To select a single cell, place the mouse pointer on the left or top border (the pointer becomes an arrow) and click the mouse.

To select an entire row, position the pointer on a column boundary in the desired row until the icon changes to a left arrow and double-click. Triple-clicking will select the entire table.

To select an entire column, position the pointer on a row boundary in the desired column until the icon changes to an up arrow and double-click. Triple-click to select the entire table.

Double-clicking on an individual cell will cause all of the cells from the current one to the end of the table to be selected. Quadruple-click the mouse to select the contents of all the cells in the table (*not* the table itself).

If the pointer is not on a column or row boundary, clicking has the following effects:

- Single-clicking places the I beam on the text within the cell.
- Double-clicking selects the current word.
- Triple-clicking selects the current cell contents.
- Quadruple-clicking selects the current cell to the end of the row.

To Move in the Table

You can use these special keys to move between table cells:

Tab	Moves to the next cell; to insert an actual tab, press Ctrl+Tab
Margin Release (Shift+Tab)	Moves to the previous cell; to insert an actual Margin Release, press Ctrl+Shift+Tab
↑	Moves up one row
↓	Moves down one row
→	Moves to the next character or column
←	Moves to the previous character or column
Home Home	Moves to the first cell in a row
End End	Moves to the last cell in a row

To Edit a Table's Structure

1. Choose Layout ➤ Tables (Ctrl+F9) to make changes in your table structure.

2. Choose one of the following options:

Join   Combines selected cells into a single cell.

Split   Splits the current cell into multiple cells. Indicate the number of either Columns or Rows you want the cell split into. Then, click OK or press ↵.

Insert   Inserts columns or rows before the current cell. Enter the desired number of columns or rows, and click OK or press ↵.

Delete   Deletes columns or rows starting with the current cell. Enter the desired number of rows or columns to delete, and click OK or press ↵.

To Format a Table

With Layout ➤ Tables ➤ Options (Ctrl+F9,O), you can edit the structure and attributes of the entire table. After editing, click OK.

Change the size of your table by entering new values for the number of Columns and Rows in the table.

Adjust the settings for Cell Margins to determine how close to the edge of a cell a value will be displayed.

Indicate the position of the table by choosing one of the following options:

- Left to left-justify the table.

- Right to right-justify the table.

- Center to center the table on the page.

- Full to fill the entire width of the page.

- From Left Edge to specify the table's distance from the left edge of the page.

Select whether negative numbers will be indicated by either a **M**inus sign, such as –378, or **P**arentheses, such as (378).

Indicate the level of background shading in the table by selecting **S**hading and entering a value from 0 to 100 percent (100 percent is black).

Enter the number of header rows to be displayed from the beginning of the table whenever a table spans a page break in the **A**ttributes text box.

Cell locks, which prevent new information from being entered into a cell, are disabled by selecting the **D**isable Cell Locks check box.

To Format Table Components

You can format individual cells, rows, columns, and lines by selecting the appropriate choice from the **L**ayout ➤ **T**ables menu (Alt+F9), making your formatting selections, and clicking OK.

Cell Formatting   Choosing **C**ell from the menu enables you to format the current cell selection.

Change the cell's appearance by choosing a combination of the following choices: **B**old, **U**nderline, **D**ouble Underline, **I**talic, **O**utline, **S**hadow, Small **C**ap, **R**edline, and Strikeout.

To change the size of the cell's contents, choose **S**uperscript, Sub**s**cript, **F**ine, **S**mall, **L**arge, **V**ery Large, or **E**xtra Large.

Check **S**hading to turn on shading in the cell.

Check **L**ock to prevent new information from being input into the cell selection.

Check **Ig**nore Cell When Calculating to prevent the cell selection from being included in table math calculations.

Cell Justification (text position horizontally) and **A**lignment (text position vertically) can be set. To use the same justification as the rest of the column for the current cell selection, select Use Column Justification. Any conflicting options in the rest of the window will automatically be disabled.

To set the selection to the same size and appearance as the rest of the column, select Use Column Size and Appearance. Any conflicting options will be disabled.

Column Formatting
Selecting Column from the Layout ➤ Tables menu (Ctrl+F9) enables you to modify column structure.

The Appearance and Size selections in the Column window are the same as those for cells.

Select Column Justification to set the justification of cells to Left, Right, Full, Center, or Decimal Align. Decimal Align aligns values with the decimal point centered in the column.

Enter the Column Width in inches or the units of measure you are using.

Enter the number of Digits that should be displayed after the decimal point.

Row Formatting
Selecting Row from the Layout ➤ Tables menu (Ctrl+F9) lets you change row characteristics.

To set the number of lines per row, select Single Line to force the row to only one line, or MultiLine to allow the row to expand when another line is added to the row.

To set the row height, select Auto to set the row height automatically, or Fixed to force it to remain a certain height (enter the row height in inches).

Line Formatting
Select Lines from the Layout ➤ Tables menu (Ctrl+F9) to select the size and appearance of the lines separating cells in the table.

Choose the line set you wish to modify, either **L**eft, **R**ight, **T**op, **B**ottom, **I**nside (of a selected range), or **O**utside (of a selected cell or range).

Set the line appearance by selecting either **N**one, **S**ingle, **D**ouble, **D**ashed, **D**otted, **T**hick, **E**xtra Thick, or **M**ixed.

To Perform Calculations in a Table

You can make calculations in a Table, using formulas with cell references as in a spreadsheet program. The referenced cells may or may not already contain values when you enter a formula.

1. Place the insertion point in the cell where you want the calculated result to appear.

2. Choose Layout ➤ Tables ➤ Formula (Ctrl+F9,F)

3. Type a formula into the text box and choose OK.

4. If you have not already done so, enter numerical values in the cells that have formula references.

5. With the insertion point within the table, choose Layout ➤ Tables ➤ Formula ➤ Calculate (Ctrl+F9, A).

● OPTIONS

Formula   Enter a formula for the highlighted cell in the Formula text box. Formulas may reference other cells and may contain numbers and operators. Calculation occurs from left to right unless you group terms with parentheses. (By contrast, most true spreadsheet programs use the standard mathematical order of precedence, with multiplication and division occurring before addition and subtraction.) Formulas containing cell references are adjusted automatically when you move, copy, or delete cells.

Copy Formula   When you enter a formula, or choose a cell containing a formula, you can copy that formula into adjoining cells in the same row or column, or copy it to a different cell than the current selection, taking into account the relative position of those cells to those involved in the formula.

To copy the formula down in the column, select **Down** and enter the number of cells you wish to fill.

To copy the formula to the right in the row, select **Right** and enter the number of cells to fill.

To copy a formula to a different cell, select **To Cell** and enter the desired cell reference.

Press ↵ to copy the formula to the selected cells, or select **Cancel** to return to the table without making any changes.

Math Operators and Functions

Formulas can include the standard mathematical operators: + (addition), − (subtraction), * (multiplication), / (division). In addition, WordPerfect assigns special functions to certain symbols that can be entered alone in a cell:

+   Subtotal: Adds the numbers directly above the cell containing the +

=   Total: Adds the *Subtotals* directly above the cell containing the =

*   Grand Total: Adds the *Totals* directly above the cell containing the *

● **NOTES**   You can also define a table using the Table icon button on the ruler.

The document window status line shows the current cell and any formula and special formatting it contains.

When creating tables from existing text, choose Tabular Column when tabs separate columns of text and hard returns define rows.

Choose Parallel Column when parallel column definitions define columns and hard page breaks define rows.

Each table is assigned a number (e.g., I, II, III) using the same numbering sequence as graphics table boxes.

Tables aren't allowed in newspaper or parallel columns (or vice versa), but you can place the table in a graphics box which, in turn, can be placed within (or across) columns.

See Spreadsheet Link for information on importing spreadsheet information into tables.

Use the document window as usual to insert, change, and delete text and graphics within table cells. Most WordPerfect features are available, including footnotes, endnotes, font, graphics, cross-reference, index, primary merge commands, table of authorities, table of contents, and lists.

● **EXAMPLE**   Figure 16 shows a sample table.

See Also   Border Styles, Columns, Cross-Reference, Font Attributes, Graphics and Graphic Boxes, Justification, Lists, Merge Operations, Move, Ruler, Selecting Text, Spreadsheet Link

I N V O I C E				
PART NO.	DESCRIPTION	QTY	PRICE	EXT. PRICE
A-1000	Onyx	5.0	$100.00	$ 500.00
B-2500	Ruby	3.0	$900.00	$ 2,700.00
X-1000	Diamond	1.0	$2800.00	$ 2,800.00
			SUBTOTALS	$ 6,000.00
			TAX	$ 360.00
	*** PLEASE PAY THIS AMOUNT *** Thanks for shopping with us!			$ 6,360.00

Figure 16: A sample table

TABS

WordPerfect gives you two ways to set tabs: from the menu system or with the ruler. You also have the choice of several tab styles.

To Set Tabs

1. Position the insertion point where the new tab setting should take effect.

2. Choose Layout ➤ Line ➤ Tab Set (Shift+F9,T).

3. Choose the tab type by selecting Left Align, Center, Right Align, or Decimal Align. If you want dot leaders (…) inserted when you press the Tab key, select the Dot Leader Tabs check box.

4. Choose the Position of the tab by entering the distance from the left edge of the document or the left margin, or by choosing a position from the list. Choose Left Edge or Left Margin to choose the location from which the tab position is measured.

5. Choose Set Tab to set a tab at the desired location.

6. Click OK or press ↵ to accept the new tab settings and select Cancel to return to the document when making changes.

To clear the tab set at the desired location, choose Clear Tab.

To clear all tabs from the ruler, choose Clear Tabs.

To return the ruler to the default tab settings, choose Default.

To evenly space tabs across the ruler, starting with the selected position, select Evenly Spaced. The Repeat Every text box opens and you must choose the default or type in another measurement. Then choose Set Tab and OK.

To Set Tabs with Ruler

Figure 17 shows the tab area of the ruler, which indicates margins, tab stops, and column positions (if the insertion point is in a column or table).

You can set these types of tabs:

- Left: left aligns text at tab stop (default)
- Center: center aligns text at tab stop
- Right: right aligns text at tab stop
- Decimal Align: aligns decimal points on the tab stop

The tab types in the ruler are the four triangular icons in the lower left portion of the ruler, and are arranged in the same order listed above (Left, Center, Right, and Decimal Align).

The button to the left of the tabs switches between standard tabs and dot leader tabs. When you click on this button, the icons are underlined by dots. Select this button before setting tabs with dot leaders.

To set tabs using the ruler:

1. Select **View ➤ R**uler (Alt+Shift+F3), if the ruler is not already displayed.

2. Drag any tab stops you wish to remove off the ruler.

3. Change the position of any tab stop by dragging it to a new location.

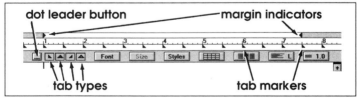

Figure 17: The tab ruler

4. To add a tab to the ruler, drag the icon for the desired tab type from the Button Bar portion of the ruler into the tab set area. Place the tab icon where you want the new tab stop, and release the mouse button. Or, hold down the Ctrl key and drag an existing tab icon of the desired type to the new location and it will be duplicated.

5. Change the alignment type of an existing tab stop by dragging the appropriate icon to the tab location.

● **NOTES** Use tabs or indents, instead of spaces, whenever you need to align vertical rows of text or indent text by a precise amount of space. Tabs are initially set at every 1/2 inch.

Tabs indent to the next tab stop, with text wrapping back to the left margins. Indents temporarily change the left or left and right margins, with text wrapping to the tab stop (see the Indent command reference).

Tabs move to the next cell in tables, or to the next level in outlines.

See Also Center, Decimal Alignment, Display Pitch and Font Adjustment, Flush Right, Indent, Initial Codes, Outline, Styles, Tables

THESAURUS

The Thesaurus lists and substitutes synonyms (words with the same or similar meaning) and antonyms (words with the opposite meaning) for words in your document.

To Look Up a Word

1. Position the insertion point on a word you want to look up.

2. Choose **Tools** ➤ Thesaurus (Alt+F1). If the word you chose is in the Thesaurus, WordPerfect will list words with similar or opposite meanings.

3. To replace the word in your document with a word from the list, highlight the word in the list and select **R**eplace. To look up a new word, choose **L**ook up and enter the new word in the Word box. To return without changing the original word, choose **C**lose.

• OPTIONS

<< and >> | If you have more than the three lists of synonyms that the screen can display, these buttons let you scroll back and forth between them.

Dictionary | Allows you to specify another Thesaurus dictionary file if you have purchased and installed one.

Edit | Allows you to cut, copy, and paste between the Word text box and the Clipboard.

History | Displays a list of the words you have most recently looked up.

• **NOTES**   The Thesaurus screen displays headwords, references, and subgroups. A *headword* is a word you can look up. *References* are are divided into nouns (n), verbs (v), adjectives (a), and antonyms (ant). References marked with a bullet (•) lead to additional headwords and references. References may be divided into *subgroups*, which are groups of words that share the same basic meaning.

If you wish to look up a reference word marked with a bullet, double-click on that word. The Thesaurus will move to the next column to display the listing for that word.

To activate a different column, click the mouse on the new column, or press ← or →.

To scroll to references *within* a displayed column, use the mouse or the vertical cursor movement keys.

See Also   Speller

TYPEOVER

While WordPerfect is in the Typeover mode, the characters you type replace existing characters.

To Activate Typeover Mode

- Press the Insert (Ins) key.

● **NOTES**   When WordPerfect is in Typeover mode, the bottom left corner of the screen displays **Typeover**.

WordPerfect is normally in Insert mode, in which the characters you type are inserted at the insertion point and existing characters are pushed to the right.

In Typeover mode, characters you type *replace* existing characters with new ones, with these exceptions:

- Typeover mode does not type over codes, which are instead pushed to the right as in Insert mode.

- The Tab key moves the insertion point to the next tab stop, and does not insert a tab space. The Tab key does insert a tab space if no text exists on the line.

- Shift+Tab moves the insertion point to the previous tab stop in the text or inserts a margin release if the insertion point is already at the margin.

- The spacebar replaces the character following the insertion point with a space.

- The Backspace key replaces the character or code to the left with a space, instead of shifting trailing text to the left.

To return to Insert mode, press the Insert (Ins) key again.

You can undelete typed over text, if necessary.

See Also   Codes, Delete Operations, Insert, Undelete

TYPESETTING

The Typesetting options include many of the features of desktop publishing and typesetting applications, giving you precise control over the final appearance of a document.

To Adjust Typesetting Features

1. Move the insertion point to where the typesetting options should take effect.

2. Choose Layout ➤ Typesetting.

3. Select the desired options (see Options).

4. Click OK.

• OPTIONS

Word and Letter Spacing The word and letter spacing options include:

Normal (word) or Normal (letter)	Spaces words or letters according to the specifications set by the font or printer manufacturer
WordPerfect Optimal (word) or WordPerfect Optimal (letter)	Spaces words and letters according to the specifications that WordPerfect considers best
Percent of Optimal (word) or Percent of Optimal (letter)	Allows you to specify the spacing width by entering a percentage of the Optimal setting
Set Pitch (word) or Set Pitch (letter)	Enables you to specify the pitch in characters per inch; this is converted to a percentage of Optimal

Percentages greater than 100 increase spacing between words or letters; percentages less than 100 decrease spacing. Larger pitches decrease spacing between words or letters; smaller pitches increase it.

Justification Limits   By default, WordPerfect will fully justify text by compressing or expanding the word space to no less than 60 percent and no more than 400 percent of normal (i.e., the space that would appear without justification). If these limits produce unsatisfactory results, use this option to adjust them.

To adjust compression, select Compressed To, and enter a percentage (0–100) for compression.

To adjust expansion, select Expanded To, and enter a percentage (100 or greater) for expansion (1000 or more enables unlimited expansion).

Once a word spacing limit is reached, spacing is adjusted between characters.

Line Height (Leading) Adjustment   These options set the distance between lines separated by soft and hard returns.

Select Between Lines to adjust the distance between lines in the same paragraph (i.e., lines that are separated by a soft return [SRt] code).

Select Between Paragraphs to adjust the distance between paragraphs (i.e., lines separated by a hard return [HRt] code).

Underlining Spaces and Tabs   To enable the underlining of spaces in underlined blocks, mark the Underline Spaces check box.

To enable the underlining of tab spaces, select the Underline Tabs check box.

Kerning   Kerning reduces excessive white space between letter pairs. Mark the Automatic Kerning box to enable the Kerning of characters.

You can also manually kern individual pairs of letters in the document window. To do so, position the insertion point between the two letters you wish to adjust. Choosing Layout ➤ Typesetting and select the Manual Kerning option. Enter the Amount of desired space between the letters, adjusting the Units (Inches, Centimeters, Points, or 1200^{ths} of an inch) if necessary, and click OK.

Printer Commands　Printer commands are codes in a document that control a printer's operation. WordPerfect's printer
drivers generate these codes automatically when you select formatting and typesetting options, so you will rarely—if ever—need to
use these codes yourself. But for projects like printing thousands of
invoices, they may improve speed. And a few printers may have
features not otherwise available through WordPerfect.

Place the insertion point at the appropriate spot in your document
before selecting **Printer Command.** Then select **Command** to enter
the codes yourself (consult your printer's manual for the correct
codes) or **Filename** to download them from a file you specify.

Baseline Placement for Typesetters　The *baseline* is an
imaginary line drawn along the base of the characters of a line.

The default typesetting method is for the *top* of the first line of text
to be aligned with the top margin. If you would like to ensure that
the bottom of the first text line appears in the same place regardless
of font or style, select the **First Baseline at Top Margin.** This will
cause the *bottom* of the first text line to be even with the top margin.

● **NOTES**　Use the Print Preview screen or print your document
to see the precise effects of changes made here. Settings not sup-
ported by the selected printer are ignored.

To restore any of these settings to the defaults, choose **View ➤
Reveal Codes** (Alt+F3) and delete the appropriate code.

See Also　Advance, Codes, Initial Codes, Justification, Line
Height, Print Preview, Printer Select, Units of Measure

UNDELETE

The Undelete command enables you to restore deleted text (including any codes within that text). WordPerfect retains the last three
deletions, and you can display or restore any one of them.

To Undelete Text

1. Position the insertion point where you want to restore the deleted text or codes.

2. Choose **E**dit ➤ U**n**delete (Alt+Shift+Backspace).

3. The most recent deletion will appear in reverse video.

4. Choose **R**estore to restore the highlighted text (initially the most recent deletion).
Choose **P**revious to display the next oldest deletion. Choosing **P**revious again displays the second oldest deletion while choosing it a third time displays the most recent deletion. Choose **N**ext to display a more recent deletion than the currently displayed one. Choosing Next on the most recent deletion will display the oldest deletion in memory. Select **C**ancel or press the Escape (Esc) key to return to the document window without restoring.

● **NOTES**   While in the document window, you can undelete any of the last three deletions as long as WordPerfect isn't in the process of carrying out a command. Use Undelete if you accidentally deleted text or codes, or to quickly move or copy previously deleted text or codes.

A *deletion* is any group of characters and codes that you delete *before* moving the insertion point to another place in your document.

You cannot undelete paired codes (e.g., [Bold On] or [Bold Off]) deleted with the Delete or Backspace key. Other codes can be re-stored. You can restore paired codes if you deleted them by another method (e.g., deleting the block of text in which they were located).

After you make three deletions, the oldest is removed from memory on the next deletion. When you exit WordPerfect, all dele-tions are removed from memory.

See Also   Cancel, Delete Operations, File Manager, Selecting Text, Undo

UNDERLINE

The Underline command toggles the underlining of text.

To Turn Underlining On and Off

1. Position the insertion point where you want to start or stop underlining, or highlight text you wish to underline.

2. Select Font ➤ Underline (Ctrl+U).

● **NOTES** Use the Layout ➤ Typesetting command to enable or disable the underlining of spaces and tabs.

See Also Font Attributes, Initial Codes, Typesetting

UNDO

The Undo command reverses the most recent change to a document.

To Undo an Operation

● Choose Edit ➤ Undo (Alt+Backspace).

See Also Undelete

UNITS OF MEASURE

WordPerfect uses measurements to position text and graphics on a page. In addition, the display window status line displays the vertical and horizontal position of the insertion point according to the unit of measure.

WordPerfect allows you to specify measurements in inches, centimeters, points, or 1200ths of an inch.

To Change the Default Units of Measure

1. Choose File ➤ Preferences ➤ Display.

2. Select Display and Entry of Numbers to set the unit of measurement in the document window and in dialog boxes. Select Status Bar Display to set the unit of measurement in the Status bar. Units of measure are inches, centimeters, points, and 1200ths of an inch.

3. Click OK.

• NOTES   Inches are the default unit of measure.

Whenever WordPerfect prompts for a measurement, you may enter either fractions or decimal numbers.

When you *omit* the unit of measure, WordPerfect automatically assumes the default units. To temporarily override the default unit of measure, *include* the units of measure letter (e.g., **12p** for 12 points); the number will automatically be converted to the default unit of measure.

Although WordPerfect only displays up to 3 numbers to the right of the decimal point, it actually calculates up to 6 places.

See Also   Document Window, Environment

WIDOW/ORPHAN

WordPerfect's Widow/Orphan Protection feature prevents one line of a paragraph from being printed by itself at the top (widow) or bottom (orphan) of a page.

To Turn Widow/Orphan Protection On or Off

1. Position the insertion point where protection should take effect.

2. Choose Layout ➤ Page ➤ Widow/Orphan (Alt+F9,W).

● **NOTES** Widow/orphan protection prevents awkward page breaks. Other ways to keep groups of lines together include the conditional end of page and block protection (see the Page Breaks command reference).

See Also Initial Codes, Page Breaks, Selecting Text

WINDOWS

The Window pull-down menu, and various buttons and borders on windows, let you open, close, size, position, and select windows. WordPerfect for Windows runs in its own application window. Each document you edit is in a document window (see Figure 18).

To Size and Position Windows

Table 14 summarizes the mouse and keyboard buttons and techniques for sizing and positioning windows.

To Switch Document Windows

• Choose the document that you want to switch to by opening the Window menu, and highlighting the appropriate document name or pressing the window number.

To Switch Application Windows

If multiple applications are running, you can use the Task List to choose a different application:

1. Press Ctrl+Escape, or choose Switch To from the Control Menu.

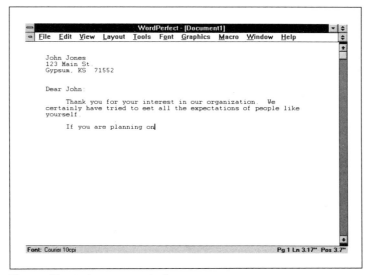

Figure 18: A document window

Table 14: Mouse and keyboard techniques for sizing and positioning windows

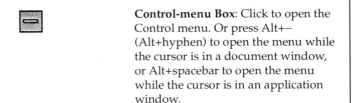

Control-menu Box: Click to open the Control menu. Or press Alt+– (Alt+hyphen) to open the menu while the cursor is in a document window, or Alt+spacebar to open the menu while the cursor is in an application window.

Table 14: Mouse and keyboard techniques for sizing and
positioning windows (continued)

Window Border/Corner: Position
mouse pointer until a double-headed
arrow appears, then drag the
border/corner in the direction that
you want to size the window.
Optionally, choose Size from the
Control menu, use the arrow keys to
size the box, and then press ↵.

Maximize Button: Click to expand
window to full screen. Or, choose
Maximize from the Control menu.

Restore Button: Click to restore a
minimized window to its original size.
Or choose Restore from the Control
menu.

Minimize Button: Click to reduce the
window to an icon. Or choose
Minimize from the Control menu. To
expand an icon to a window, double-
click the icon, or press Alt+Tab until
the icon is highlighted, and then
release all keys.

Scroll Bar: Click on the up or down
arrow to scroll, or drag the scroll box
to new location, or click anywhere in
the scroll bar. Optionally, use the ↑, ↓,
PgUp, PgDn keys to scroll vertical
bars; or the ←, →, Home, End,
Ctrl+PgUp, Ctrl+PgDn to scroll
horizontal bars.

Title Bar: To move a window, drag the
title bar at the top of the window to a
new location. Or open the Control
menu, select Move, use the arrow
keys to position the window, and
press ↵.

2.   Double-click the application you want to switch to, or use
     ↓ or ↑ to move the highlight to the application name and
     press ↵.

To Rearrange Windows

1.   Choose **W**indow from the WordPerfect for Windows main
     menu.

2.   Choose **C**ascade or **T**ile. Cascade overlaps open document
     windows so that each title bar is visible. Tile arranges the
     open windows in smaller sizes using a tile-like setup, ena-
     bling you to see every open window at one time.

● **NOTES**   The File ➤ Open command opens a new document
window, with its own status line and tab ruler (see the Retrieve command reference). File ➤ Close (Ctrl+F4) closes an active window (see
the Save/Save As command reference). You must activate (click on)
a window before you can edit its contents. The title bar of the current
(active) window is usually colored differently from the other (un-
selected) windows.

See Also   Dialog Boxes, Document Window, Menus, Retrieve,
Save/Save As

WORD COUNT

The Word Count command counts the number of words in document or selected text.

1.   If you want to count words in only a portion of your docu-
     ment, select that text.

2.   Choose **T**ools ➤ Word Count.

3.   WordPerfect counts the words, and displays the result in a
     window. Click OK or press ↵ to return to your document.

Index

WordPerfect 5.1 Compatible Keyboard Shortcuts

	KEY	SHIFT+KEY	ALT+KEY
Esc	Cancel		Next Application
F1	Help	Preferences	Thesaurus
F2	Search	Search Next	Replace
F3	Undelete	Next Document	Reveal Codes
F4	Indent	Double Indent	Select
F5	File Manager	Date/Outline	Mark Text
F6	Bold	Center	Flush Right
F7	Close	Print	Tables/Columns
F8	Underline	Layout	Styles
F9	End Field	Merge	Graphics
F10	Open	Save As	Macro Play
F11	Reveal Codes	Ruler	Draft Mode
F12	Select	Select Cell	